C000104593

In Their
OWN
Words

INTERVIEWS WITH WOMEN IN JAZZ

Sammy Stein

8TH HOUSE PUBLISHING

8th House Publishing
Montreal, Canada

Copyright © 8th House Publishing 2020
First Edition

ISBN 978-1-926716-59-6

All rights reserved under International and Pan-American Copyright Conventions. No part of this book may be reproduced in any form or by any electronic or mechanical means, including information storage and retrieval systems, without permission in writing from the publisher, except by a reviewer, who may quote brief passages in a review.

Published worldwide by 8th House Publishing.
Front Cover Design by 8th House Publishing

Designed by 8th House Publishing.
www.8thHousePublishing.com

Set in Garamond, Raleway and Caslon.

LIBRARY AND ARCHIVES CANADA CATALOGUING IN PUBLICATION

Title: In their own words : interviews with women in jazz / Sammy Stein.
Other titles: In their own words (2020)
Names: Stein, Sammy, 1962- interviewer.
Description: Includes index.
Identifiers: Canadiana 20200366734 | ISBN 9781926716596 (softcover)
Subjects: LCSH: Women jazz musicians—Interviews. | LCSH: Jazz musicians—Interviews. | LCGFT:
   Interviews.
Classification: LCC ML385 .I35 2020 | DDC 781.65092/52—dc23

Author's Introduction

Women are a formidable presence in jazz. They are finally getting well-deserved respect for their contribution to the music, both on stage and behind the scenes. Women bring with them qualities which add to the music, creating a richer, more diverse art form. For decades, women have fought for their place in jazz. Early female pioneers in the industry forged new paths through a sea of misogyny, sexism and ignorance. The benefits of those pioneering women are being harvested by those in the industry today.

Yet for all that, women still have battles to fight; subtler today, yet still intrinsic to jazz. Female jazz musicians are gaining ground, step by step, and finally we are heading toward the day when musicians are chosen for nothing other than their talent.

This book contains interviews with female musicians who have made it on the jazz scene. They share their stories. We meet women with decades of experience and those with just a few years performing behind them. Some specialize solely in jazz whilst others also play other genres. All of them have followed their hearts and inner visions, sometimes in the face of extreme adversity.

I have interviewed many people. As time has passed, more and more women have told me about their journey through jazz. I wanted to give these women a voice—a place where they could speak freely and tell their stories. The women interviewed come from a range of cultures, different backgrounds and ages. Their different characters are discernible in their responses. Some talk at length, and include asides, anecdotes and illustrations of points whilst others give short but still complete answers somehow.

These women have all been reviewed and written about. The Internet holds a lot of information on them, but these interviews reveal what search engines can't. They correct some misconceptions and explain choices made. We hear about events that helped shape them and their feelings on many issues. What sparked their interest in jazz? What drives them?

Deciding who they want to be and finding how to get there can be difficult for any woman. Many paths have been made easier with improvements in education and equal rights. Societal changes have had a profound effect on how women are perceived, their expectations of themselves and how others view them.

Audiences, readers and listeners are so much a part of every musician's journey. It is my hope that the reader will both enjoy these interviews and also learn more about the struggle each woman underwent to follow her dreams, push forward and achieve success in jazz music.

So, who will you find in this book? You will find Sheila Jordan, who is in her tenth decade and truly an icon of the jazz scene. She has been present whilst the jazz industry has undergone some of its most profound changes. Jane Bunnett is noted for her collaborations with Cuban artists and her advocacy of female musicians. Arema Arega is an Ethiopian-Cuban-Spaniard whose journey is quite unique and involves her art as well as her music. There is Barb Jungr who never ceases to amaze with her different takes on composers like Bob Dylan, Bob Brel and Leonard Cohen as well as her own composing and arranging.

Then there is Melissa Aldana, a Chilean tenor saxophone player, now living in the US and award-winning vocalist Georgia Mancio, arranger of the famed 'Hang' events in London and one of the most respected vocalists in Europe. There is Silvia Bolognesi, an Italian double bass composer, arranger and performer. Shirley Smart is a cellist who has enjoyed success both in the Middle East and Europe. Taeko Kunishima is a Japanese piano player who blends traditional Japanese music into her playing style and collaborates with players of traditional Japanese instruments like the *shakuhachi*.

Tina May has been a prominent singer on the European scene for many years and here too, is Brandee Younger who, as a harpist, has found success in the US and Europe. There is Camille Thurman an award-winning saxophone player from America who plays with the Jazz at *The Lincoln Center Orchestra* and performs as a solo and collaborative artist and Mimi Fox, a renowned guitar player whose playing is respected across the globe. There is UK singer, composer and multi-instrumentalist Julia Biel, and Ellen Andrea Wang, a double bass player who has created her own distinct sounds.

We also meet vocalist, drummer and cabaret star Kitty La Roar and Ginetta Vendetta, a trumpeter described as 'a triple threat' due to her singing, playing and composing. Then there is Millicent Stephenson, an award-winning, influential saxophone player and founder of the empowering Cafemnee, and Selina Albright, an outstanding and successful vocalist from the US. There is Alison Rayner, an award-winning bass player, record label co-owner and composer and Isabel Sorling, an improviser and vocalist who is becoming an important part of the European jazz scene. These are influential, powerful women who are making the journey a little easier for those who follow their lead.

The women discuss being in a business still largely dominated by men, the differences they are noticing. They talk about hot flushes, menopause and other specifically female issues; combining motherhood with being a musician. Some discuss finances, offer advice for anyone thinking of coming into jazz and insights into managing the business side of things. They discuss travel, new initiatives and fellow female performers.

The interviews were carried out many ways due to the busy lives of the musicians interviewed. We called; we used messaging services; we sent sound bites back and forth; we e-mailed, met before or after gigs and of course arranged face to face meetings specifically for interviews—events which invariably involved cakes and maybe a drink or two.

Their stories are fascinating and need to be heard. These are just some of the many women now very present in jazz and in their words we hope to understand what those journeys have involved. For some, the road has been relatively smooth; for others there have been moments when the pressure has been relentless and the behaviour of others towards them mortifying. But here they are, giving interviews, sharing their stories.

Contents

In Their Own Words
Interviews with Women in Jazz

Selina Albright

"Every element on the stage is important—the attire, the lights, the sound, the musicians, the material. And when we all find that groove and flow with it, it's magic. It's spiritual. It's delicious. It's transformational!"

"People are being forced to think differently about the definition of gender— to explore why they may feel alarmed by changing gender norms in the entertainment industry. It's tough to make people change their opinion of topics on which they've built their whole concept of reality and codes of conduct!"

"I don't intend to change and grow alone. I want us all to grow and be uplifted together, and I hope my music facilitates that in some way, even if for just a few of you! Every song is my whisper to you that you're more than enough, you're not alone, life is to be celebrated, and I thought about you while I was creating this."

Selina Albright grew up steeped in jazz history. She is the daughter of saxophonist Gerald Albright and a popular singer who can turn her talent to most genres. She attributes her onstage charisma and vocal techniques to being exposed to legendary artists, such as Whitney Houston, Ella Fitzgerald, Tina Turner, Dinah Washington, Beyoncé, Lalah Hathaway and Tina Turner. Since 1997 she has contributed to her father's projects. Selina wrote and performed the lyrics of the title track for Gerald Albright and Norman Browns' *Grammy* nominated album '24/7' (Concorde 2012). She was also featured on Peter White's 2016 release 'Groovin'. Most recently, Selina made a feature appearance on Jarez's 'Blow Your Mind'. Her solo works include the R&B/Soul 2013 release 'Brighter' which topped the UK Soul Chart for four weeks, and her sassy 2010 Jazz original 'You and I' which was featured on iTunes' 'Top 100 downloads' list for jazz in 2010. Her 2016 single release 'Sun Comes Up' primed the market for her 2017 full-length R&B project 'Conversations' which received wide acclaim. Selina has also enjoyed success in collaboration with electronic dance artists including the internationally revered DJ duo *Manufactured Superstars*. In 2011 an estimated 200,000 people watched as they performed 'Serious' for the Las Vegas *Electric Daisy Carnival*.

Selina has performed with world-renowned artists including Joe Sample, Brian Simpson, Nick Colionne, Norman Brown, Marcus Miller, Dave Koz, David

Sanborn, Kirk Whalum, Steve Cole, Boney James, Hugh Masakela, Chaka Khan, Will Downing, The Temptations and Pieces of a Dream to name just a few.

In this interview, Selina shares her experiences, her ideas about sharing music, her pride on being a young night owl, guidelines on stage collaborations and a lot more.

The Selina Albright Interview

Who would you say influenced your early life—not just in music but you as a person?

SA: The influences in my life—the people I look up to—are my father, who taught me the importance of diligence and perspective in and beyond the music industry; my mother, who taught me to be an individual and not worry about others' opinions and expectations of me; my grandmother, who kept me grounded in a close relationship with God, and my huge village of extended and adoptive family members, who taught me how to love without condition.

Musically, my influences are Ella Fitzgerald, Dinah Washington, Billie Holiday, Miles Davis, Gerald Albright, Erykah Badu, Whitney Houston, Mariah Carey, Lalah Hathaway, George Duke, and Tina Turner. This is in no way, a complete list.

What was life like as the daughter of Gerald Albright, a prominent musician himself? Do you think there was ever doubt you would follow into music?

SA: Being the daughter of a prominent musician was unlike many other childhoods one would consider 'normal', but I didn't know that, because the experiences of my childhood created my definition of 'normal'. I interacted with celebrities other kids wouldn't normally have access to. I was introduced to night clubs and concert halls as a baby and taught how to behave while my father was performing. I was brought along to countless recording studios where Dad would work and I got to experience the practice and focus behind the development of his technical skills and unique sound firsthand. I was a proud 'night owl', when other kids had to be in bed by 8:00pm. I was rarely allowed to get my clothes dirty, because, as my mom repeated many times, I was, 'representing the family every time I leave the front door.' It was a lot of pressure, but it groomed me.

My parents knew that I had talent and promise as a musician as early as when I was just two, but they never forced the issue of me becoming a musician professionally. Instead, they made sure that the necessary tools for all my interests were at my fingertips, so that I could decide my own passions freely. All I knew from the beginning was that whatever I did, I wanted to be my own boss. So, I first prioritized finishing school, earning my degrees and securing a backup plan. Then I searched my soul to find my true passions. I was determined not to be a 'starving artist'. Of course, when I felt the time was right to pursue music full-time, my parents were very proud and supportive! (And I still haven't missed a meal yet.)

Can you tell me what drew you to soul and jazz?

SA: I naturally gravitated toward what I was exposed to the most. From a young age, I heard my father's music regularly, and friends of the family would gift me jazz CDs—anything from Ella to Coltrane to Thelonious. In my impressionable teenage years, the Neo-Soul era swept the world, and I heard artists like Maxwell, D'Angelo, and Erykah Badu change music with their new ideas! I'm a product of all those experiences, and while I successfully dabble in other genres of music collaboratively, I believe that there have been no genres that better fit my vibration as an artist.

Can you describe how performing makes you feel, and what you like about it?

SA: Imagine being good at baking. You never went to culinary school for it, but somehow you have a knack for one favorite dessert that your family and friends always ask you to make when you all get together, because nobody makes it the way you do. You go to the store and you gather all the best ingredients in the proper amounts. You sift, pour, stir and fold until their collective consistency is just right to your taste. You've made this recipe many times but each time, you add something just a little different or change the balance just a little to try and perfect it more with each new preparation.

Now imagine that you, yourself, are the secret ingredient to this recipe and you add yourself—all of you—to this recipe every time you make it. You complement and blend with the other ingredients in such a way that once the temperatures and the rhythm and timing are just right, it's irresistible and you become immersed within it.

Then, you set the dessert under a spotlight and offer it to those who already know and love the taste of it and to some who've never had it before but have only heard, and you all indulge together and get transported in flavor and texture.

That's how it is for me to perform. Every element on the stage is important—the attire, the lights, the sound, the musicians, the material… And when we all find that groove and flow with it, it's magic. It's spiritual. It's delicious. It's transformational!

What is the music scene like in the US jazz in particular? When you have toured other countries is there a marked difference in demographics, ages coming to gigs?

SA: The jazz scene truly depends on where in the U.S. you find yourself. Places like New York, Los Angeles and New Orleans definitely have a stronger jazz presence than other areas. Then you have cities like Denver, where the scene is just starting to bloom. I find that the jazz demographic is from a more seasoned age bracket than myself, so I consider it nothing short of an honor that jazz lovers in the U.S. have received my music well.

Interestingly, when I travel to other countries, there is a much wider age range at each concert. People will travel three hours or more to see me live and are more likely to bring their children and parents along.

How do you find the difference playing large and small events? Do you have a preference?

SA: As my dad always says, no matter how big or small the audience it's our duty to give the same level of showmanship and musicianship. Everyone in that audience bought their ticket and showed up for us, so it's only right that we show up for them! I perform by that standard to this day.

I really don't have a preference when it comes to audience or event size; there are benefits to each. I care more about audience enthusiasm and connection. Sometimes, the smallest venue can have the wildest energy! I give everything I have whenever I perform, and when the audience is feeling it, I dig down and somehow find even more to give! I love the connection that music allows me to have with the audience and get a kick out of seeing the connections being formed between audience members while we're all experiencing this musical event together.

How important is collaboration between you and musicians? Do you like to control how they interpret your song writing or do you assign them strict lines?

SA: I do set certain guidelines for the sake of form and cohesion on stage and in the studio, but collaboration between myself and the other musicians is very important to me. I tend to be more inclusive of other musicians' styles when they show up well-studied and ready to flow. This way, there is a common trust among us all. I learn so much from hearing what the musical voice of another artist brings out of me. With the right musicians, I even sing my songs a little differently from what I'm used to. That's where the real fun of collaboration comes in.

What's most important is that I collaborate with the right artists—ones who will challenge me, those who will be comfortable bouncing ideas and energy between one another, who are open to improvisations in styles they haven't tried before. When a collaboration is like this, we can all be free to add our unique contributions to the overall feel of the music. Something new is organically created—it's a beautiful thing, and I believe the audience feels the music more when everything about a performance isn't rigidly choreographed.

How do you choose who to work with? What are you looking to find in their playing which would make you want to work with them?

SA: Many times, I'll meet another artist unexpectedly, whether we first meet performing at a jam session or at a group recording session. And once I hear their musicianship and begin to feel a kindred spirit of sorts, it makes me want to play together again.

I naturally gravitate toward other artists who tend to 'geek out' about music, are super professional and focused, and have a warm, humble heart. If a musician feels like family to me, chances are, we'll end up working together more in the future. Everyone I call to perform with me on stage is a person

I also consider a friend or adoptive family member. This makes for richer musical experiences across the board.

Are there other events in your life which have affected your music? Do you think going through major events in life are useful for musicians or do they make you close down emotionally?

SA: I'm the type of songwriter who uses the writing process as therapy. Writing helps me to emotionally process those major, life-changing events. I find that being fully present in life and embracing my passionate nature—good and bad—fuels my song writing capabilities. For this reason, and for my own self-awareness and self-growth, I welcome all new and unknown things to happen to me. It's a win-win.

I've dealt with everything from deep elation and gratitude, to tragic loss, to growing pains, to marital bliss, to having to encourage myself after being judged harshly. It may be a vulnerable position to put myself in—allowing the public to hear my deepest of thoughts and the emotions that I'm not proud of—but the benefit of releasing the emotional strongholds, and of helping others not to feel alone in their triumphs and tribulations, makes the exposure worth it.

Do you feel that there is still a harder path for women in music? Is this changing and so you see a future where gender will not be an issue? Do you feel the US is more difficult for women than anywhere else?

SA: It's amazing the grip that patriarchal, outdated societal norms continue to have on the arts, an entity that by nature should promote and protect freedom of expression for all who choose to take part in it!

My stance: A woman's 'proper place' in music must become solely a personal choice, a reflection of her experiences, gifts, and aspirations—not a place decided by society or tradition. I feel that there will always be a few conflicting opinions and preferences about a woman's 'proper place' in music, wherever you are in the world. However, gender limitations are being challenged and broken over time, especially with blurred gender lines being progressively more accepted the world over. People are being forced to think differently about the definition of gender—to explore why they may feel alarmed by changing gender norms in the entertainment industry. It's tough to make people change their opinion of topics on which they've built their whole concept of reality and codes of conduct. So yes, women still have a tough road ahead, but we're doing it!

The proof of this paradigm shift is in the rising number of females who are unapologetically redefining the entertainment industry and taking it by storm. It's an exciting time to be alive!

Can you see changes happening in jazz music—are audiences growing, is there a thirst for more adventure in music do you feel?

SA: I see jazz being more infused with other genres these days. I find that many artists will use traditional jazz as a theoretical foundation, and then apply to it the key elements of other genres. The late George Duke had a strong presence in funk, R&B, and contemporary jazz. Newer artists, such as Esperanza Spalding and Robert Glasper, are channeling anything from rock to Latin, funk to old school, fusion to avant-garde, and blues to R&B when they compose. Lines are being blurred and the focus is becoming more about musicianship. Jazz artists are now free to offer the musical response to the questions: What elements truly sound good together that we haven't put together before? What combinations of sounds can reach audiences in a way they've never experienced before? How can we marry two or more opposites? Do we really care to fit into one genre at a time?

If you could meet your younger self—just about thinking of a career in jazz music, is there any piece of advice you might give her?

SA: Yes. I'd tell her to continue to study her craft, but not with the goal of perfection. I'd tell her to connect to how she feels, more than how she sounds to others and what others might think of her.

What would you like to say to people who listen, come to shows and buy your music?

SA: I'd like to say that I'm always changing, and that's intentional. I'm aware that the music industry has defined my genre in at least three different ways over the years, and that this may throw some creatures of habit for a loop. Call it adult ADD, but I like it that way. I enjoy the process of growth, movement and rebirth, deeply enough that I refuse to limit my path. I could be anything new tomorrow. In fact, I'm counting on it!

I don't intend to change and grow alone. I want us all to grow and be uplifted together, and I hope my music facilitates that in some way, even if for just a few of you! Every song is my whisper to you that you're more than enough, you're not alone, life is to be celebrated, and I thought about you while I was creating this.

Lastly, I love and appreciate every one of you for sticking with me through every twist and turn. There are songs and lyrics that almost didn't make it to the airwaves, because I thought they'd be too 'this' or too 'that'. But you embraced them anyway. THANK YOU!!! You haven't gone unnoticed. I couldn't continue to create if you stopped supporting this dream of mine, because I don't think you truly realize. This. shit. is. expensive. So, thanks again.

Sheila Jordan

"...the cops were always stopping me and taking me down for questioning about hanging out with Afro-American kids. Even my principal in high school gave me the third degree for my choice of friends. It was terrible but I knew I was right and their opinions were wrong."

"I feel more and more women are getting involved in jazz music and are not as intimidated as in the earlier years."

Sheila Jordan commands huge respect both in her native United States and across the globe. Born in Detroit, Michigan in 1928, Sheila was working in clubs by the time she was a teenager. Her influences were Charlie Parker and other instrumentalists. Sheila faced stiff opposition to her career choice and the company she kept, largely from the white community. She was part of the trio *Skeeter, Mitch and Jean* with Skeeter Spight and Leroy Mitchell. Her husband, Duke Jordan, was Charlie Parker's piano player and she studied with Lennie Tristano. In the early 1960s she made her first recordings using her voice more like another instrument. Again, she faced disapproval. Vocalists of the time were expected to sing lyrics—especially female vocalists. Many people came to appreciate Sheila's musical talent however and she made more recordings during the 1970s.

Sheila has received many awards. A very few are the *Bistro Award for Outstanding Contributions to the Art of Jazz; The International Society of Bassists Recognition Award for Collaborative Music; Jazz Education Network Award for Outstanding Performance; National Endowment for the Arts Jazz Master Award—Lifetime Honors Award* (America's highest honor in Jazz); *The Mary Lou Williams Women in Jazz Award for Lifetime of Service;* the *Lil Hardin Armstrong Jazz Heritage Award.* There are many more awards. Sheila loved the idea of doing an interview for this book and I found a lively, warm and willing interviewee with a lot to tell and more than a touch of humour. She talks about, among many other things, racial prejudice, her experiences with Lennie Tristano and Charlie Parker, thoughts on jazz education, other women in jazz, and drugs.

The Sheila Jordan Interview

Thank you for agreeing to be interviewed.

SJ: Here goes. I'll do my best.

Sheila, who were your major influences—not just in music but on you as a person?

SJ: Charlie Parker from fourteen on. Mr. Usher, my piano teacher in my first year of high school—that's about it.

What attracted you to jazz?

SJ: The soul and rhythm of it. I heard Bebop at fourteen and that was it. I was hooked.

When you started out, how did you deal with the disapproval shown towards you by members of the community?

SJ: The racial prejudice in Detroit, Michigan was very, very bad and the cops were always stopping me and taking me down for questioning about hanging out with Afro-American kids. Even my principal in high school gave me the third degree for my choice of friends. It was terrible but I knew I was right and their opinions were wrong.

When you first started, I am guessing there was still a fair bit of male dominance in the jazz music world. Did this affect you?

SJ: I really never got into that too much. I just wanted to be around the music and most of this music was played by men. Women hadn't gotten to the point where they are in today's world. The singers were accepted—Billie, Sarah, Ella, Anita, but not the instrumentalists. If women played an instrument, however, I always saw them being encouraged by the male musicians.

Charlie Parker famously dubbed you, 'The Singer with the Million Dollar Ears'. What was he like?

SJ: I never worked *with* Charlie Parker. That was my husband Duke Jordan. I only sat in with him if he asked me to do a song. It wasn't a *gig* though. I just sang a song or two once in a while when he asked me. When he heard me sing, he always complimented me and encouraged me. He called me, 'the kid with the million-dollar ears' after hearing me in Detroit at a jam session.

Lennie Tristano has always interested me because he was an incredible innovator and improviser. I understand you learned with him. What did you gain from him?

SJ: He was a great teacher and very encouraging. He had a lot of students and after our lesson on a Saturday night, he would have a jam session where everyone played and I sang. I was the only singer he taught. He usually only taught instrumentalists. Charlie Mingus and Max Roach told me about Lennie when I told them I was looking for a teacher. Lennie taught me to be myself and to learn the song the exact way it was written i.e. lyrics, time, melody.

How does jazz in the US compare with the scenes outside the US? You have travelled and performed internationally—is jazz well received in most places?

SJ: I find through my years of touring that jazz is much more accepted in Europe than the U.S. They don't even mention it anymore on the *Grammy Awards* for example. It's like it doesn't exist. It's a shame too because jazz music is the only music America can call its own. I call it, 'The Step Child of American Music' because of its lack of acceptance.

How do you see the future for jazz?

SJ: As long as teachers and performers like myself are out there keeping it alive it has a good chance of surviving. I teach and encourage my students to do the same as I did. It's such a beautiful art form.

Are there any changes which you feel need to be made in the music industry where women are concerned or not? Have things changed much since you started?

SJ: I feel more and more women are getting involved in jazz music and are not as intimidated as in the earlier years. I love it when I go on a tour and there are women accompanists in the group. I just worked with a wonderful young woman drummer in Slovenia. She was swinging and sensitive and she listened.

If you could meet your younger self, just starting in jazz, is there a piece of advice you would give to her?

SJ: Yes, I would tell my younger self not to drink or take drugs. They don't make you sing better; in fact, they make you sound worse and can ruin your voice. The same holds true for instrumentalists. You might think you sound better but it's not true. You're ruining yourself.

You worked, I understand, with young people at City College, New York for many years. How did you find the young peoples' approach to jazz?

SJ: I started the first vocal workshop at City College in 1978. I did a little concert up there and the great John Lewis from the *Modern Jazz Quartet*, the head of the jazz department, Ed Summerlin and the classical voice teacher Janet Steele all approached me after the concert and said I should be teaching there. Since I didn't have a degree in music, I really felt unqualified and told them my feelings and that I wasn't schooled to teach. They all told me to teach what I do and that's what I have been doing since then—teaching my approach, etc. I am very grateful to each one of them.

How did I find their approach to jazz? The kids were very interested. I started a two-week workshop at the *University of Massachusetts* in Amherst at the insistence of Max Roach and Dr. Billy Taylor. This was in the early '80's and it is still going on. It is called 'Jazz in July' and takes place the first two weeks of July. I also started a one-week workshop at the *Vermont Jazz Centre* in Putney and it is still going on and very successful. I have had some wonderful students throughout the years and some have gone on to become quite successful.

Do you feel education, along with the introduction of jazz degrees, more courses aimed to attract young people, women and minorities into music, jazz and the arts is having an impact?

SJ: I feel any music program featuring jazz and blues is very, very important in schools. I know the workshops I do now when I am invited to different universities are very successful and the students really get into the music. Hey, it's American music that has been overlooked. Let's be proud of it and keep it alive.

How did you come to work with Georgia Mancio? It was she who introduced us.

SJ: I met Georgia in London, I believe; and she is a wonderful talent. Her singing, writing and performances are of the finest quality. She's a great example of one of the special people keeping jazz alive. She has written some wonderful lyrics and I believe recorded with the great Alan Broadbent. It's been a while and I have a tendency to forget at this tender age of almost 91. Sorry about that but Georgia can tell you more.[1]

Is there anything you would like to add?

SJ: All I want to say to the young jazz folks or old jazz folks is keep singing, don't give up something you love. Support it until it supports you. It might never support you but why give up something that is part of your soul?

---

1 SS—she does—see later

Tina May

"Women in jazz, just as in society, have suffered historically. Sexism and misogyny existed and is well-documented especially in the early days. Women were and still are objectified. As the years have passed by, though, some women have broken through."

"I want to take people on a journey, emotional, lovely, sad or happy, surprising, edgy."

Tina May is frequently billed as one of the best European vocalists. She has toured and gigged with nearly everyone who is anyone in the music business and is very popular in the UK and Europe. She works as both leader and with other musicians. Her list of past and present collaborators is impressive and includes Don Weller, Clark Tracey, Nat Adderley, Joe Henderson, Nikki Iles, Alan Barnes, Ray Bryant and many more. She has played across London and Europe in festivals, halls and smaller venues. As well as singing, she has been in major productions of musical theatre as well as being an author, article writer and Variety Councillor of the *Equity Council* and a liveryman of the *Musicians Company*. Tina remains one of the most popular singers in Europe and it was an honour that she found time to give thought to answering my questions. Here she talks about Europe, childcare, her long term relationship with *33 Jazz Records, Equity* and much more.

The Tina May interview

Who were your early influences?

TM: I grew up in a very musical family. They were amateurs in the true sense. My mother had a lovely voice and played piano—light classical but mainly songs from the shows.

She was a very significant influence and I used to enjoy singing with her from a very early age. Dad also played the piano—mainly stride à la Fats Waller. Listening to Dad play was where I first realized that jazz was huge fun to sing and dance to… 'Your Feet's Too Big' etc. I loved family parties where we all played and sang around the piano. My sister, Viv played violin and I used to play the clarinet. Dad was a Scot and we regularly spent Hogmanay in Scotland with the many aunties and uncles—where singing your 'party piece' was *de rigueur*.

Making music became a natural thing to do in our household—everything from folk music— Scottish, English, and American—to popular songs by Sinatra and Doris Day. My Mum loved Ella Fitzgerald, Duke Ellington and Count Basie. We used to dance around the room.

Rhythm and dancing to music was the most natural thing because my parents were very good ballroom dancers. That's how they met. They used to tell stories of the dance bands they would go and listen to, going to London, dancing all night, catching early trains home… I certainly inherited a *joie de vivre* from Mum and her voice, too.

SS: How did you get into jazz music?

TM: I already loved jazz and had listened to a lot in my childhood and teens. However, my father was pretty terrified at the idea of his daughter going into show business and refused to let me go to a drama or music college. I was not the sort of kid who would go against his wishes—especially as my mother had tragically died just as I was going on to further education. So I read French at Cardiff University doing a BA (hons) degree as I had always loved the French language and *chansons*.

My lovely Mum had encouraged my singing and I studied classical singing from the age of 16 onwards finding a fabulous teacher named Eileen Price, whilst studying in Cardiff. Eileen was lovely and let me sing Duparc, Fauré, Debussy—they were all my favorites and very jazz!

Had my mother not died perhaps I would have studied music and drama but I couldn't fight Dad, and besides, I inadvertently found myself in a wonderful place for live music. I joined the *Welsh Jazz Society* in the first week of university and met like-minded musicians. I saw all the great touring jazz musicians, as Cardiff was on the circuit.

As I was studying a language, the third year was spent abroad. I applied for Paris as I knew they had wonderful jazz clubs. I was right!

Why did you decide to stay in Paris after studying there?

TM: On the first week in Paris, I met some young jazz musicians who became long term friends. Patrick Villanueva is a pianist and Pascal Gaubert a tenor sax player with whom I have recorded two albums for *33Records*—'Live in Paris' (2000) and 'No more Hanky Panky' (2011). They were playing with the *Roger Guerin Big Band*. I started singing with this band. In the drum chair was the one and only Kenny Clark. I got to sing with him a lot that year, also with Georges Arvanitas and Dany Doriz, the French Lionel Hampton. It was a blissful time for me and I nearly didn't come home to the UK.

I was also fortunate to meet and work with a stellar talent of comedy, Rory Bremner, and that summer we took a musical revue to *Edinburgh Fringe*. Jazz and comedy work very well. I sang Bob Dorough/Dave Frishberg's 'I'm Hip' à *la* Blossom Dearie—I am a life-long fan. Ever since those days I have worked in Paris and all over France. France and, in particular, Paris is my spiritual home.

So, I got my degree in French and went straight into a touring theatre job as an actress. I had already acquired my Equity union card through jazz singing contracts. Musical theatre is a life-long passion, so I was quite employable.

I joined a French-speaking theatre company called *Bac to Bac,* which zigzagged between Paris and London but were based in London—that got me to London. I had vowed not to go to London without gigs or theatre employment. The French came in handy after all! In fact, many years later in 2008-2009, I played and sang the main role of Liza Elliot in the 1941 Jazz Broadway musical 'Lady in the Dark'[2] with the orchestra of the *Opera de Lyon* and *Théâtre la Renaissance* which toured throughout France.

I was involved in musical reviews and broadcast projects for the next five years—a great privilege.

You moved to London—why and how did that go?

London is so much bigger than Paris. I made good friends with some great musicians quickly, especially at the old *606 Club* in Fulham and, of course, Ronnie Scott's. The eighties were very good for gigs in London. There were some pretty hip places where people were rediscovering jazz music and dancing. These places were not like the *Caveau de la Huchette*, but nevertheless, it was

---

2 Moss Hart, Kurt Weill/ Ira Gershwin

great! I was a busy singer and felt really lucky. I even sang chansons in a little place called 'La Vie en Rose'. Happy days.

You have a long association with 33 Jazz Records—the story goes you sent in a demo, the label called you and offered you the chance to record—is this correct and how did it feel?

TM: Fast forward a few years. I was married and a Mum to my little son Ben, who was a year old. I was living out of London, not far from Luton where there was an arts centre called *33 Arts Centre*. I sent a demo cassette in 1990, hoping for a gig and Paul Jolly of the record label associated with the arts centre offered me a recording contract! I was over the moon and still am! It was so unexpected and so very welcome. I needed to keep creating and singing. It would have been easy to stop being a professional singer. Everything is against you, particularly childcare issues. I still woke up with music in my head, even though I was now a Mum. If it had not been for my Dad, who now was totally supportive of my singing, I don't think I could have carried on. He would come and stay when I had a week at Ronnie Scott's Club and help out. He was a truly wonderful Granddad.

Paul Jolly has always been a true friend to jazz music and its musicians. He supports but never tries to dictate what you record and is always involved in the recording process in a positive way. He is a dear and very genuine person (also a saxophonist). I am blessed to have him as a friend and colleague. He also has a great sense of humour.

What about other countries—is jazz music well-received?

TM: I have extensively toured in China and find that they are very enthusiastic about the music. When I sang in the *Shanghai Concert Hall* people were dancing in the aisles. There are a lot of young musicians coming up and I feel there is a growing love of the genre which is very heart warming. Australia has produced many great jazz musicians too. Generally, they need to leave Australia and work in Europe and the States to get enough work unless they diversify in genres. I ran across Mark Fitzgibbon, a wonderful pianist from Melbourne, when I sang in Shanghai. I first met and worked with him in London in 1985! It is a small world, indeed.

In general, on festivals the demographic is pretty wide. In Paris, there are still many more jazz festivals throughout the year than in London. Jazz has long been adopted by the French as their music—which is why so many jazz musicians who visited from the States, like Kenny Clark, never went back home. They were made welcome and didn't suffer the racism they experienced in their own country. France hosts many jazz festivals large and small, from hot club, bebop and techno swing to New Orleans throughout the year.

There is a radio station called *TSF* dedicated to jazz music twenty-four hours. On *France Musique* and *France Culture*, live jazz is broadcast regularly. There is much more jazz content on radio, film and television in France. Germany has many festivals and big bands. This is because of a commitment to arts sponsorship. In fact, all over Europe there is a real commitment to the Arts.

How does being a mother fit in with your musical career?

TM: Juggling motherhood and a career is always difficult, not just for musicians. As long as you have support you can get through. As I mentioned, without my father's help, I couldn't have toured and kept going. If you have a supportive partner—that will help. I am divorced and brought up the children pretty much on my own. We survived and the children are happy, successful adults. We made some amazing memories together all over the world—as I always tried to take them with me on interesting trips abroad. Ben went to Hong Kong and Australia and Gemma remembers snow in Central Park when we premiered the Ray Bryant Songbook at the *Jazz Standard*, New York. It was her eighth birthday! She recently came on a trip to Shanghai just before she went away to university. In many ways they saw more of me than if I worked nine-to-five as I was often around in the day time.

You are involved with Equity as a variety councillor—what does that role entail and why do you feel equity is important?

TM: I am involved in *Equity*, the entertainment union. I believe in professional unions passionately—for everyone's wellbeing and safety. Actors and musicians are very vulnerable to exploitation, after all. We love what we do.

Why jazz vocals?

TM: Singers are generally expressive storytellers and songs are stories. In jazz we take the story further every time we perform and build on it with improvisation. This brings constant renewal and a sense of 'now' in our performances. There are definitely life events that deepen your understanding (love, loss, motherhood, friendship, hardship) and this can only give you a greater palette of emotional colour in the music you make. Singing and songs can be very 'healing' experiences for the audience and singer alike. I think people react in a very visceral way to a voice—it hits you in a way that is sometimes more direct that instrumental music. Of course, we also sing lyrics of great beauty and power. Jazz music for me is life affirming and very vital.

Do you feel there is a harder path for women in jazz music? Is this changing and do you see a future where gender will not be an issue?

TM: Women in jazz, just as in society, have suffered historically. Sexism and misogyny existed and is well documented especially in the early days. Women were and still are objectified. As the years have passed by, though, some women break through.

Singers have always been around but I mean bandleaders and instrumentalists like the Ivy Benson band in the forties, Carla Bley, Maria Schneider—we see few of them but gradually and surely, they are on the rise. It seems to me that every generation becomes less tolerant of sexism in the music industry -and yet we still have a fight on our hands because the music industry is still, generally, run by men.

More women are getting involved in production and recording and this gives me hope for future artists. Music, and in particular, jazz crosses all boundaries. In my opinion when there are more female producers and visible women arts practitioners, seen and heard on all media outlets then we will have real change. On the barricades, girls! See you all there!

You have been involved in Education such as the Tuscany summer schools and elsewhere. How do you feel European musicians are faring? Some countries like Italy appear to have funding crisis, is this correct and how is it affecting music?

TM: Jazz Education is really important to me. I am passionate about it. We should hand on our experience and help the upcoming generations. When I was growing up you could see and hear jazz on television on a Saturday night.

At peak time viewing Cleo Laine had a wonderful show with many guests. It was really a great thing for so many kids who had a chance to encounter jazz music. I was one of them. You could hear jazz everywhere on radio. Nowadays you have to seek it out—which makes it more obscure.

When I started my career there were also many more places to play, [to] learn your trade and 'pay your dues'. There were many more venues that offered live jazz music.

I set up a jazz summer school in France 2003, 2004, 2005. This was very successful. Since then I have taught in Tuscany and Paris, also Coaraze near Nice. Summer schools are a great way of having a concentrated, fun experience for a week or two. I would always recommend this and I always offer workshops when touring abroad. It's really useful for students to work with you in the afternoon and then come to a gig and watch/ listen to your performance. A lot of things start to make sense that way... There is no shortage of great young musicians. We are training wonderful, creative, talented performers. We now need to make sure the venues and festivals celebrate this and market it. We have great singers, composers, songwriters, instrumentalists and society needs to nurture them.

How do you feel young people find jazz? Is there an enthusiasm for it and do you think education specifically in different genres is vital or not so much?

TM: Young people, like any generation, react positively to live music and jazz in particular. Recent films like 'La La Land 'have got young hipsters dancing to jazz again. The *Caveau de la Huchette* in Paris is packed with young people. It doesn't take much effort to get them through the door, then they're hooked.

If you could meet your younger self—just about thinking of a career in jazz music, is there any piece of advice you might give her?

TM: I think I would urge myself to 'believe in myself' a little more and occasionally assert myself a little more, get angry (not 'put up' with things so much).

Given a blank canvas, just Tina looking at the listening and interested world, what would you like to say to people who listen, come to gigs and buy your music?

TM: As far as my music is concerned, I want to take people on a journey, emotional, lovely, sad or happy, surprising, edgy. I relish the celebration of life in all its colours in my music and lyrics. From 'A Flower is a Lovesome Thing', to Chet Baker's Solo on 'Night Bird', Ray Bryant Songbook, to 'Café Paranoia' and celebrating the fabulous Mark Murphy...Piaf...I continue with forthcoming Duncan Lamont Songbook recording this January 2020 plus my recent project called *Three Wishes* and *52nd Street Stories*. I can't wait for new adventures in jazz!

Isabel Sorling

"There's actually a name for the Scandinavian jazz sound. We call it "fjälljazz" (mountain jazz), which has a clear connection with our vast natural landscapes. This style of jazz music is characterized by open large soundscapes and minimalistic melodies."

"Playing music is very addictive to me. It feels like my third leg. For better or worse, to be a musician feels like my purpose on this earth."

"As everything in our western communities our societies gets more and more commercialized, and I'm truly disturbed by how this is affecting music."

Isabel Sorling is a vocal improviser, composer and musician, born in Ulricehamn in Sweden 1987. An up and coming star of the improvised music world, she now lives in Paris. Isabel is an artist who freely navigates the boundaries between improvisation, folk, and avant-garde, blending vulnerability with mastery. Here she discusses growing up in a small town, the joys of good education, moving to France and knowing her purpose and more.

The Isabel Sorling Interview

SS Who would you say influenced your early life—not just in music, but you as a person?

IS: I grew up in a small town, the youngest child of five with separated parents. Neither of my parents had a big interest in music, so I mostly heard the radio while I was growing up. Ever since I was young, I sang to myself, trying to repeat the melodies that I heard on the radio. It was my sacred 'room', being inside music. I was always drawn to live music, whenever I had the chance, through events at school for example.

I spent a lot of time at my grandparents' house, and my grandfather was always an inspiration to me. He was always very curious and had a great sense of humor. He had his father's old violin at home that he tried to play, with his old, crooked hands. But he had a great appetite for music and sharing these moments with him was very dear to me and inspired me to play.

When I was 15, I met my mother's father for the first time, and he turned out to be an accordion player. Fortunately we did one or two concerts together before he passed away. At this age I was already beginning to play gigs at weekends. A friend and I started a duo and played at local places, like churches, libraries, weddings, markets, fairs, and we eventually became our own sound technicians. This experience was a first insight on what working as a musician meant.

In 2008, I met the fantastic vocal teacher named Ingela Hellsten as I started studying improvisation at Gothenburg University. I'm forever thankful for what she taught me. She gave me freedom. She taught vocal techniques that gave me access to my voice and she encouraged me to take risks. That gave me the vocal freedom, to explore and sing whatever I heard in my head. It made it possible for me to improvise without boundaries.

She was an inspiration to me. She had a way of treating and respecting you as a professional musician—quite in contrast to my experience in my little hometown, where choosing music as an occupation was not seen as a serious career path.

Can you tell me what drew you to jazz?

The freedom in improvisation. I felt that I had found 'my' language. I had a group of friends, we were about 17 years old, and we started to play jazz in school. We took those first steps into this new-found music genre together. There was no competitiveness among us, and we didn't think of jazz as hard, or something we couldn't or shouldn't do, so we had a free run discovering jazz music.

As I was the singer I always felt that the frame for a classic jazz singer didn't interest me. I was told that jazz singers scat but I couldn't find myself in that sound, so for a while I improvised on the piano instead. I was never particularly interested in being the front musician, and as a singer, you're often in front, so now when I look back, I can see how I always shied away from that position, trying to be in the back just doing my thing, but still being in the music. It was when I began to think of my voice as an instrument that I felt much more comfortable. I had found my place on stage.

Can you describe how performing makes you feel/what you like about it /the sounds/connection/anything?

IS: On stage, while improvising, I enter into a flow. It feels as if I'm one with my intuition. Small decisions are being made constantly I tend to change and do whatever is needed for the music. Sometimes I kind of zoom out, hearing the music from the outside, while being in the middle of it. And then I zoom in on the other musicians' sound.

I love how music takes over me and kidnaps my other senses. Everything else disappears. I feel as if I leave the room and go to another universe. Those journeys are very strong and thrilling. I used to be very shy, but being on stage always felt like my safe place, where I could express myself.

What is the music scene like in Sweden and jazz in particular?

IS: I think that due to the fact that Sweden is a small country with a lot of space and nature, it affects the music itself and also the music scene. There's a big focus on exporting. We're quite eager to spread our music outside of Sweden. That being said, musicians that are active mostly on the Swedish scene tend to stick to their communities. But I've also seen an urge from the young jazz musicians to do cross over projects with other music styles.

There's actually a name for the Scandinavian jazz sound. We call it *fjälljazz* (mountain jazz), which has a clear connection with our vast natural landscapes. This style of jazz music is characterized by open large soundscapes and minimalistic melodies like the sound of *ECM* artists Bobo Stenson and

Jan Garbarek.

I have realized, while living outside of Sweden, that Sweden has a big singing tradition. Many people have sung or sing in choirs, in school for example. Maybe this is because of our protestant churches. We also sing on parties and celebrations—it comes from our pagan traditions. So our jazz singers are often very anchored in folk and choir singing.

I understand you studied in Sweden but are now based in Paris—why the move?

IS: By coincidence. This French journey began when I was studying improvisation in Gothenburg. I heard about the possibility to do an exchange year in a different country. I happened to be in France on vacation the very day I had to choose between different schools, so I chose Paris.

What was supposed to be six months travel to France has become a now nine year travel and it is still ongoing. After traveling back and forth for many years to play with all the French projects but while still being based in Sweden, I finally moved permanently to Paris two years ago. It was out of a practical reason. My heart is still in Sweden.

That being said, as France is in the middle of Europe, it's much easier to explore and take part of the international scene, which has always drawn my curiosity.

How do you find the difference playing large and small events? Do you have a preference?

IS: I like the mix. For me, switching the size of the venues keeps me awake, and makes me aware of the space I'm performing in. I like working with and exploring every different room and audience.

But I do have a special love for apartment concerts, when you're really next to the audience. Then you're so close that you can feel the audience's energy and take part of their detailed expressions. And the conversations afterwards I find are always very interesting. Often at a house concert the division between artist and audience are minimized, which allows people to really meet and discuss what music is and what emotional impact it has.

One of the things that is interesting playing on big stages is the technical advantages. I played with a circus for many years, often in front of 2000 people. With the technical possibilities we could create a magical room with electrifying effects. And when the mass of claps and shouts comes back to you from the audience, it hits you with such power.

I also love playing in rooms that are not made for concerts. Like in mines, or outdoor industrial sites. It's very interesting to investigate a space and explore the different possibilities, and work with the room instead of against it. I find these occasions very creative and musically stimulating.

You collaborate with other instrumentalists, particularly those on the improvisation scene. Are there any projects which have a special place in your heart and why?

IS: I value each musical meeting. It's very interesting and exciting to get inside another musician's sense of time and flow. This investigation is endless. And still you can understand it instantly.

Since 2010 I have been part of the Scandinavian sextet *Farvel*. It's the group that I've been playing with the longest. We've spent countless hours playing, rehearsing, exploring together; and as a result, the musical connection and sense of group sound is very deep. Another group very engaging is *Soil Collectors*. We are kind of an artistic collective, with the richness of different art disciplines, always doing everything with an experimenting mind.

And last, in 2019 I became part of a big improv ensemble; *Tropic*. With nine musicians from Europe, Scandinavia and North and South America, led by French guitarist Julien Desprez and the American trumpet player Rob Mazurek. This international meeting is naturally very interesting, and the soundscape possibilities seem boundless. It's a wild haven of explosions and interactions. With all its raw energy you just have to throw yourself into the music, and be fearless.

For me these groups are an endless laboratory, which I love. They push me to explore.

Are there other events in your life which have affected your music? Do you think going through major events in life are useful/good for musicians or do they make you close down emotionally?

IS: Well, your state of mind and your life are naturally connected to the music you're playing.

Even during my hardest times, I've still been wanting to go on stage, because on stage I enter into just 'being'. Thoughts disappear and a performance has a way of cleansing your spirit.

I'd say that at major events in my life, I'm so happy that I've chosen my passion for my work. It gives a meaning of life, a pursuit of exploration that never ends. That being said, the lifestyle of a musician takes a lot of energy, emotionally and physically. And you're constantly traveling. I sometimes ask myself what it would feel like, to have an ordinary lifestyle, not having to work with my passion. One year ago I almost changed my career path and my life. It was in a moment of a lot of questioning. I finally realized though, that I couldn't stop the music. Playing music is very addictive to me. It feels like my third leg. For better or worse, to be a musician feels like my purpose on this earth.

Do you feel there is still a harder path for women in jazz music? Is this changing and do you see a future where gender will not be an issue? Is Europe / Sweden more difficult for women than elsewhere do you feel?

IS: I've seen how the gender equality on the jazz scene has changed slowly since I began twelve years ago. Today there are many more female instrumentalists active on the European scene, and there's less focus on them being women, and more on their music. I can still see differences between countries. The attitude and understanding is in general much more advanced in Sweden then France, for example. Sweden made great efforts in developing a more equal jazz scene, with for example a 50-50% gender rule on most jazz clubs (vocalists not withstanding in the count). Not everyone was happy about these quotas, from both genders, but I think it was a necessary tool, during the short time it lasted, to open up and change old habits. "Gender" was also added as a course on our university program, which led to it becoming a subject that was intensely discussed. As a result I see that the landscape looks different than from ten years ago. But there's still a lot of work to be done to reach a gender equal presence on the music scenes.

Can you see changes happening in jazz music—are audiences growing,

is there a thirst for more adventure in music do you feel?

IS: I'd say that there's a lot of crossover between genres and musicians that's going on right now. Lots of jazz musicians take their craftsmanship of improvisation into other genres and try to create something new out of that.

The habits of listening to music is somewhat changing now with this new streaming era. Especially for the young audience who only stream. Playlists are being labeled after what mood or utility you need music for. For example sport, dinner, party. I think this might twist the purpose of music around and really affect the music creators in general. Maybe less so on the jazz scene. I hope that people stay curious. Going to concerts without knowing what they'll hear. Buying a vinyl just because they're drawn to the cover artwork, and then discover new music.

If you could meet your younger self—just about thinking of a career in jazz music, is there any piece of advice you might give her?

When I were seventeen I remember that I thought long and carefully as I was deciding to choose a music career or not. It felt like an important decision and I took it with great sense of care and thoughtfulness, understanding that being a full-time freelancing musician was hard. But I was so drawn to playing music, as I never felt more full and complete then while I was inside it. So I went for it, with 100% of determination and passion. Ever since that decision, I've embarked on every project coming my way, and I've learned and experienced a lot by doing many different kinds of projects. But somewhere along the way I've felt like I've lost my own voice, by mostly being a side musician. I'm trying to give that voice time and space now. To initiate projects, compose more, researching and investigating even deeper. So if I'd have a conversation with a twenty-five year old version of myself, I would encourage her to take time to also initiate her own projects and musical ideas.

Given a blank canvas, just Isabel looking at the listening and interested world, what would you like to say to people who listen, come to gigs and buy your music?

IS: Try just to feel what the music brings to you. Become one with the music. Music is such an emotional tool to enlarge all of your inner landscapes. In its own natural way, music just wants to help you feel, so let it do just that.

I've noticed that nowadays we have a tendency to get into a kind of rate mode: "Is this music good or bad? Do I like it or not? As everything in our western communities our societies get more and more commercialized, and I'm truly disturbed by how this is affecting music. I see the tendency that musicians, trying hard to maintain their position in the hard competitive music business, try to adapt their music to fit into a more sellable product. Though it's so important that musicians don't do just that. As music is this organic organism pouring out of a person, it has to be free and alive so that it can pour into someone else. However, of course we need to find a way to have the music distributed and sold. But it's up to the seller, whomever that might be. Often it's the musicians themselves. It's important to think about this today, from the perspective of a musician and of the listener. How do we want our future music to sound like, what do we expect of the industry, of the artists, of music? It's all of us who has the power of painting how we want our future music to be.

It's important that artists have the liberty to develop an artistic idea to its end, before having to think of it as a product. I think that that might be the key to keeping music as a living organism.

And if you want to support artists, keep going to live concerts and buy albums. That really does help these days, when we've gone into this streaming era, especially for all independent artists. So stay curious, stay open-minded, and set the music free.

♭ ♭ ♭

Ellen Andrea Wang

"I've always been fascinated by rhythms in music; how bass and drums make the foundation in the music and how rhythms are such a physical thing. You can feel it in your body."

"I would say that the music scene in Norway is quite unique. There are so many jazz clubs and festivals, which is amazing because Norway is such a small country compared to others. Norway has very good jazz schools where talent seems to seep out through the tap water."

Ellen Andrea Wang is a bass player, composer and musician who blends jazz and popular music. She has a rawness in her acoustic sets which is balanced by a lyricism and a mystique in her voice which is engaging. She injects an urban essence into her performances with her band. Ellen is founder of the critically acclaimed indie jazz band *Pixel* who have achieved national and international success. She has toured with French drummer and songwriter Manu Katché and Danish percussionist Marilyn Mazur's ten women strong *Shamania*. In 2016, she performed with Sting. In 2013, she introduced her own trio at the *Oslo Jazz Festival* with Andreas Ulvo on keyboards and Mathias Eick on drums.

Ellen has achieved recognition including awards such as the Kongsberg Jazz Festival's *Great Musician Award* in 2015. She is hugely influential on the Norwegian jazz scene but her fame is also spreading far beyond her own country. Reviews of her work are positive and her live performances are described in glowing terms. Adventurous in her music, Ellen has embarked on another great adventure—that of becoming a mother. In her interview Ellen discusses many things including the power of music to connect people, teachers encouraging students' creative nature, buying a double bass on a whim (and far from home), and how motherhood has tempered her views on touring. She also covers the fact that some countries give financial support to jazz music, whilst others do not.

The Ellen Andrea Wang Interview

Who would you say influenced your early life—not just in music but you as a person?

EAW: I grew up in a small village in Norway, Søndre Land. My dad is a priest and my mom is a teacher and organ player in church. They both led the choir—and still do—so I grew up singing gospel music, hymns and children's songs in the church choir. Our home was always open for people to stop by for a cup of coffee and a conversation. I've always admired my parents for being so involved and open minded to people in our community and the village. My parents use music as a cultural exchange in the church and it's has been wonderful to experience the power of music and how it connects people no matter what their skin color, gender, religion or age. I think there is something unique about singing in a choir together and being part of a collective group. There is no competition, everybody is a winner.

Growing up I had my best time at middle school with wonderful teachers, students and friends. Not just the music teachers but our teachers in general. A shout out to *Søndre Land Ungdomsskole*[3]!

I guess it's a rare thing to say but my best school years were when I was between 13 and 16 years old, with all the hormones and stuff going on (ha ha). But our teachers (Håkon and Valborg) gave us so much freedom to be creative. For example, if you had to make a presentation in geography you had the option to make a song out of it, draw a picture or use drama.

Every day at school we had to be active for 30 minutes. You could take a walk, play basketball or football. It's a physical programme named the *Fysak-programme*. Looking back, I think having teachers and a school like this is something that I'm really grateful for. Let kids be kids, let them be creative and let them play. This was a normal public school, not a private school.

I think these early experiences in life and this approach to learning gave me a fundamental understanding for what's important in my life. It gave me the freedom to see things with different perspectives and it gave me so many opportunities.

Can you tell me what drew you to jazz?

EAW: I've always been fascinated by rhythms in music; how the bass and drums make the foundation in music and how rhythms are such a physical thing. You can feel rhythm in your body. I grew up dancing to Michael Jackson's music and to Chick Corea's 'Spain'[4]. I can still recall the blue balloon vinyl cover of Keith Jarrett 'European' Quartet's 'Belonging' (ECM 1974) with Palle Daniellson on bass, Jan Garbarek on saxophone and Jon Christensen on drums, lying on top of our vinyl player at home. 'Spiral Dance' was my favorite song and it still is one of the finest songs I know. I never get tired of that album.

Jazz music has just always 'been there' in my life. My dad is, besides being a priest, also a pretty good jazz piano player so we listened to a lot of jazz vinyls at home and went to jazz concerts and festivals. I remember going to McCoy Tyner concerts at the *Kongsberg Jazz Festival* or when the Arild Andersen[5] trio

---

3   Norwegian for Middle School.

4   From his 'Light as A Feather' album 1987 Polydor.

5   Arild Andersen is a Norwegian jazz musician bassist, probably the most famous Norwegian

came to our school and played.

I clearly remember the first time I heard jazz music which was more modern. It sounded almost like the pop music I was listening to. I think I was around 14-15 years old when I discovered 'Jaga Jazzist'[6] and the album 'A Living-room Hush'[7] and Bugge Wesseltoft's[8] 'New Conception of Jazz'[9]. I remember it was a total 'A-ha!' experience because I did not know that jazz music could sound like this!

I really related to this kind of music! It wasn't like the American jazz standard swing/bop music. These bands were stretching the term 'jazz music' and inventing a different sound. It was a big door-opener for me and I still remember the feeling I had when I discovered this. It was like I had discovered the best secret ever by myself; like tasting the best ice-cream but not being able to describe the taste. It was just a part of your sensory apparatus.

Why bass? I understand you switched from violin to bass when you were young—was there a reason for this? Can you describe how playing the bass makes you feel/what you like about it /the sounds/anything?

EAW: From an early age I played both the piano and classical violin. I played in an orchestra and I also sang in choirs. I never practiced the violin much and I did not learn sheet music very well. I guess one of my strengths has been that I've always been good at playing by ear and adapting melodies when I hear them, so I would rather listen to recordings and play, than play from sheet music. It was kind of hard playing in an orchestra.

At some point I understood that I would never be better than playing 2nd violin in the orchestra and I wanted to learn more about jazz music and how to improvise.

My uncle Torfinn played the electric bass and I tried that a little when I was a teenager. The summer I turned fifteen years old, I was in Prague in the Czech Republic with a choir and I went to an instrument shop. They had many beautiful double basses so I bought a cheap double bass without knowing

bass player in the international jazz scene.

6   Jaga Jazzist is an experimental jazz band from Norway that rose to prominence when the BBC named their second album, 'A Livingroom Hush', the best jazz album of 2002.

7   Ninja Tune, 2001.

8   Jens Christian Bugge Wesseltoft is a Norwegian jazz musician, pianist, composer and producer.

9   Jazzland Recordings, 1997.

how to play it! The next morning, we were going back home to Norway by bus and I asked the bus driver if we could kindly get the double bass in the bus (with all the 50 other suitcases, ha-ha). He had to take all the suitcases out of the bus. Then we placed the double bass carefully in the luggage space and rode back to our home. On the bus trip from Prague to Gjøvik I remember I was re-defining myself from being a violin player to becoming a bass player. This was freedom for me! I wanted so badly to play an instrument that not everybody was playing and I wanted to sing as well while playing the bass. I remember the phone call I had to make to my violin teacher. It was a little hard for me but I was a bass player. I just knew it!

Going from violin to double bass, you have the same understanding of intonation—actually, let me explain that in a different way—I mean *understanding* of the instrument.

The double bass is such a physical instrument. You have to work to get the tone and the sound you want. That is something that I love about it. You have to dig into the instrument and make it sound like you want to—to the wooden sound sing.

What is the music scene like in Norway and jazz in particular? Can you compare the jazz scenes in other countries you have played in?

EAW: I would say that the music scene in Norway is quite unique. There are so many jazz clubs and festivals, which is amazing because Norway is such a small country compared to others. Norway has very good jazz schools where talent seems to seep out through the tap water. The scene in Norway is alive and it's evolving all the time. Someone told me that Oslo has the same number of concerts each day as Copenhagen and Stockholm put together! Norwegians love to go out and listen to music. Norway has around seventy jazz clubs. I don't know exactly how many jazz festivals, but there are plenty. The key to keeping a jazz scene alive is to recruit a younger audience, and to recruit a younger audience the promoter needs to book both established and up-and coming musicians/bands. Annual festivals like *Moldejazz*, *Kongsbergjazz* and *Vossajazz* give a jazz musician a commission to write new music and put together a new band to perform at the festival. Very often the musicians who receive the commission are in their late 20's or early 30's. The Norwegian jazz scene is very open-minded. It is okay to mix jazz with pop music, rock, folk, or intense noise.

I received a commission from the National Jazz Scene in Oslo last year and I put together a new dream band with Jon Fält from Sweden on drums and Rob Luft from Britain on guitar. Two both amazing musicians who I admire and had wanted to play with for a while. I wrote new music based on the aesthetics and philosophy of jazz bassist Charlie Haden. I named the project 'Closeness' and later in 2020, we will release an album and play concerts around Europe. The trumpet player Arve Henriksen will sometimes join us. He is an amazing improviser who brings so much good energy to the band.

So by having these commissions it's possible for Norwegian jazz musicians to realize dream projects.

Another important thing to mention is that the *Norwegian Culture Council* gives economic support to jazz music. From country to country there are vital differences in how much money festivals or jazz clubs have to fund their program or festival.

How do you find the difference playing large and small events? Do you have a preference?

EAW: I love both! It depends what kind of music I'm playing.

Are there events in your life which have affected your music? Do you think going through these are useful for musicians or do they make you close down emotionally?

EAW: I just became a mom for the first time! That has been a wonderful. I'm used to travelling two hundred days a year, but now I have been home with my baby girl for seven months. I will play a couple of concerts in Norway but I decided to cancel my whole European tour. As a band leader with responsibility for my band members' pay checks, I felt bad in the beginning; but now I couldn't be happier about the decision I made. Being a mum is a part of life and I really did not want to miss precious time getting to know my daughter. Tour life is like a never-ending spinning carousel; you just have to know and decide when to jump off for a while and when to jump back in.

Do you feel there is still a harder path for women in jazz music? Is this

changing and do you see a future where gender will not be an issue? Is Norway more difficult for women than elsewhere do you feel?

Very often when you get questions about gender in jazz music like, "What is it like to be a female bass player?" In the early days earlier days I would reply. "Oh no, not those questions again". But now I'm like: "YES! We need to talk about this. We have to talk about it until there is nothing to talk about."

The truth is that right now there are a lot of female bass players in Norway. And they are all really good.

I don't know if I would say it's a harder path for woman in jazz in general, since it's hard itself just living as a jazz musician, but I think that there have not been enough role models for woman in jazz. And that is one of the reasons why it has been so male-dominated. It's wonderful to see all the talented female jazz musicians coming from universities or playing in bands. I play in a jazz/pop group named GURLS. And for me GURLS is the band I wish I had when I grew up.

I don't think any of my male band colleagues has ever thought of me as a woman before a bass player. For them, I'm a bass player. But I must admit that I sometimes miss female colleagues when I'm on tour. When I was touring with drummer Manu Katché it often happened that I was the only female musician on the whole festival line up.

How do you feel jazz is treated in education—do musicians who study jazz stay in the business? Are female musicians encouraged?

In Norway jazz education is very popular. I think it's important to remember that you don't become a musician just by just studying music at a school. You become a musician when you have the motivation, will and the courage that you want to explore, learn, adapting and being creative, surrendering yourself in music.

The approach to jazz and improvised music is very important. I studied at the Music Academy in Oslo and while it's basically a jazz/improvised music education you also learn to improvise in all musical styles. It's possible to improvise in rock and pop music as well; it just has some different musical codes than jazz, for example.

Some of Norway's biggest pop stars started studying jazz at university and after graduating they wanted to write pop songs instead, and they write really good pop songs in my opinion. So I think jazz studies give you important tools in how you want to interact in music. And you can use those tools the way you want.

If you could meet your younger self—just thinking of a career in jazz music, is there any piece of advice you might give her?

Good question! I guess I would say that it's important to dive into the unknown to learn as much as possible. And don't compare yourself too much with others because there is no one who plays just like you do.

Given a blank canvas, just Ellen looking at the listening and interested world, what would you like to say to people who listen, come to gigs and buy your music?

If there was no one in the audience I could not have this dream job—so thanks to everyone who comes out to my shows and for buying my music. I never take that for granted, really!

♭ ♭ ♭

Silvia Bolognesi

"My instrument choice meant that it was really hard to play in jam sessions. If someone wanted to play on the fact I was a woman, they had to learn I wasn't kidding."

"Music has always been a social comment. I live it like a moment of sharing. The music comes out from the musicians but the audience vibes are important too."

Silvia Bolognesi is a double bass player, composer and arranger. She graduated in double bass studies at the *R. Franci Institute* of Siena, studying under Maestro Andrea Granai and later Maestro Alberto Bocini. Silvia studied at the *Siena Jazz Academy* with Paolino dalla Porta, Furio di Castri and Ferruccio Spinetti. The most significant encounters in this musical training were with bass player

William Parker, composer and musician Muhal Richard Abrams, cornet player, conductor and composer Lawrence "Butch" Morris, composer and saxophone player Roscoe Mitchell and multi-instrumentalist Anthony Braxton. Silvia was awarded the Música jazz magazine's *Top Jazz Award* in 2010 for best new talent and in the same year she won the *In Sound* trophy for double bass category. Silvia leads bands including *Open Combo, Almond Tree, Xilo Ensemble,* and *Fonterossa Open Orchestra* and is part of the international string trio *Hear In Now* with Tomeka Reid on cello and Mazz Swift on violin and vocals. She took part in the *Art Ensemble of Chicago, 50th Anniversary Special* project. She also runs her own record label, *Fonterossa Records* and teaches double bass and combo class at the *Siena Jazz Academy* and other institutions as well as being part of the European exchange organization, Erasmus and running workshops.

The Silvia Bolognesi interview

Who would you say influenced your early life—not just in music but you as a person?

SB: My older brother was definitely a big influence in my early life and also the reason I got into music, first as a lover/listener then as a player. He played in a rock band[10] and I used to follow him to rehearsals, concerts and go with him to other bands' shows. In my teenage years music was a big thing even though I didn't play an instrument. Music kind of defined me.

Why the bass? Can you describe how playing the bass makes you feel and what you like about it?

SB: I started with an electric bass—again I was influenced by my brother's scene. I started in a local band, mainly because I thought the bass was cool, groovy, dancy. I began to explore jazz more because when I was attending Siena Jazz, an historical school in my home town, someone gave me the record, 'Ah Um'[11] by Charles Mingus. The sound of Mingus's double bass blew my mind and I decided to switch to double bass. The double bass is very different from the electric. It has the same function in music but is a different tool. The thing with the size is that it vibrates a lot and it's not easy to put out sounds when you start, but when the strings started to vibrate and the sound

---

10   And still does.

11   *Ah Um*, Charles Mingus; released by *Columbia Records*, 1959.

came out it was so satisfying, it really fulfilled me. So, that was real love and I started my journey. Studying it in the conservatory and creating different sounds with it became quite a challenge, from the low, rhythmic lines to the melodies for classical concerts. It's still a challenge and I guess it always will be, but I love it!

How do you feel about young people and jazz? Do you feel there is still the interest there was a few years ago? Has it grown or diminished? Do you think education, including jazz degrees, makes a difference?

SB: I teach jazz and I question myself a lot about it. There is interest and the amount of young talented musicians is growing, at least in Italy. I think jazz education is making a difference and musicians are more prepared; but the academic path is kind of short and I believe music needs time so you can process information and deal with the instrument. Also, listening to music is very important and nowadays the approach to listening seems so different from when I was young. There was less access to music then, so we knew less probably; but we listened to that smaller number of pieces we could access a lot.

Have you ever heard someone play and been totally blown away by what you are hearing?

SB: Many times, both in records and at concerts. What I said earlier about Mingus, I had the same experience when I heard the William Parker Quartet for the first time. When I saw Muhal Richard Abrams and Roscoe Mitchell playing live I couldn't sleep for days. Many others blew my mind and mainly it was not only because of their greatness on the instrument but also for the material chosen. I care a lot about emotions in music and I guess that's what affects me the most.

How did your association with the Art Ensemble of Chicago[12] come about?

SB: In 2014, I was in California for a few concerts with the *Hear in Now*

---

12   *The Art Ensemble of Chicago* is a music group that developed from the *Association for the Advancement of Creative Musicians* (AACM) in 1968-1969. The players use many instruments, large and small and these may include bells, whistles, and horns. The players may wear costumes or make up when performing, creating a visual and aural experience. 2019 was their official 50th anniversary year.

trio—myself, Mazz Swift and Tomeka Reid. Tomeka knew Roscoe Mitchell because she had performed with him before. Mitchell was teaching at Mills[13] and we decided to go and visit him. We gave him one of our records and a few days later he emailed us saying he really liked it.

Two years later he invited us to be part of his sextet for a tour dedicated to John Coltrane. That same year the trio joined the *Art Ensemble* in London for two shows at *Cafe Oto*—that is how it started.

Are there events in your personal life which have affected your music? Do you think going through major events are useful for musicians or do they make you close down emotionally?

SB: I know people are different and react to events differently. Music has always been something to clutch on to for me. When I started studying double bass seriously I was dealing with a big loss. Major events are not useful to music, but music is useful to process them and save you. As Albert Ayler said, "music is the healing force of the universe".

What made you decide to found your own record label? Was this a huge decision and did you need to have particular business acumen to do this?

SB: My label is just for self-production, it is not a business at all. I started it because it was really hard to find a label interested in putting out my records. Nowadays you have to buy your own records from most of the labels, so I did some calculations and I found out that producing my own records had the same costs but I would have the freedom to make my own decisions and retain more control of my own music. Then under the *Fonterossa* name other records came out, without me being part of those, mainly because musicians from my scene had the same problems I had. Instead of doing other self-productions with different names we thought it would make more sense put them out under the same label. I'm actually surprised that it's working well. It takes time and can be stressful but it's worth it.

Do you feel there is a harder path for women in jazz music? Is this changing and do you see a future where gender will not be an issue?

---

13   A music school.

SB: I wanted and want to see a future where gender will not be an issue, but it's not that easy, especially in my own country. When I was younger I thought by now things would have been different and they are in a way. By that I mean there are more women in jazz, but it's still harder for women on the jazz path.

This is a big topic that I question more about nowadays, especially because I teach and I care about young musicians. When I was young I had to deal with the women issue a lot but I acted like there wasn't a problem. I guess because I cared just about music and I really wanted to keep going. But people are different and many young musicians can stop playing because of bad attitudes towards them, especially in jazz. I must say in the conservatory even though there were few women, and especially in the double bass class there wasn't that feeling of being lonely as I have found in the jazz scene.

Jazz is pretty much about showing skills, strength, being a badass which can get so tiring, so stupid and I got caught up in that when I was younger. My instrument choice meant that it was really hard to play in jam sessions. If someone wanted to play on the fact I was a woman, they had to learn I wasn't kidding, I was the real thing—like a man!!

This is really sad, but yes—usually when someone wanted to give me a compliment this was the line: "Good job, you play like a man". But I was lucky because in my path I found and chose people who didn't care. I found great musicians that I played with and still do, amazing teachers who supported me and did not make me feel different. Also, there are older women in jazz who walked that path in even harder times. They showed me it was possible.

Do you notice differences in the music scenes (especially jazz) in Italy, the US and elsewhere, even in Europe itself?

SB: Yes I do. I guess it's cultural and Italian. It's not an easy country for women in any career, even outside the music environment.

If you could meet your younger self—just about thinking of a career in jazz music, guitar in hand, is there any piece of advice you might give her?

SB: Well, I really don't know. I feel blessed because I achieved more than I was expecting in music. I didn't even think I could have done this as a profession. I guess I would advise her to do the same. Maybe I should have been less shy and responded to that line about me playing like a man by saying, "some men suck on the bass!"

Given a blank canvas, just Silvia looking at the listening world, what would you like to say to people who listen, come to gigs and buy your music?

SB: Music has always been a social comment. I live it like a moment of sharing. The music comes out from the musicians but the audience vibes are important too. I know usually we who play are on stage and we might look 'far away' but we are actually together. We rehearsed and practiced something to share with whoever is listening. It's a community moment.

Alison Rayner

"It was exactly the music I had been looking for—challenging and free—but with great grooves and wonderful melodic tunes."

"A strong ethos of the band was a feeling that we must have control. We were opposed to the commercial record industry, which we saw as driven by profit, exploitative of musicians and deeply sexist."

"I love the way the bass centers the music and holds the ground between rhythm and harmony. Everyone in the band wants to hear it because it gives them their foundation."

Alison Rayner is an award winning double bass player and composer from the UK. She was awarded an *Ivor Novello Composer Award* in 2019 and was runner-up in the *British Jazz Awards* for double bass in both 2018 and 2019. Since the 1970s Alison's career has spanned many styles and she has played internationally with musicians including vocalist Carol Grimes, trumpet player Chris Hodgkins and guitar player Dierdre Cartwright. She toured with the internationally acclaimed Latin/jazz group *The Guest Stars* throughout the 1980s.

Her quintet, *ARQ*, play contemporary jazz and have released three albums so far. They regularly play across the UK and Europe. ARQ won *Ensemble of The Year* in the 2018 *Parliamentary Jazz Awards* and were shortlisted for the *Small Group Prize* in the 2018 British Jazz Awards. Though jazz rooted, Alison's music encompasses influences from a broad musical palette and the media—and audiences—love this inventive musician.

Since 1989, Alison has co-run *Blow the Fuse*, an artist development partnership based in London. Through this, she has performed with artists including guitar legend Tal Farlow and New York poet Jayne Cortez, saxophonist Peter King and guitarist John Etheridge. She acknowledges the support of her fellow musicians in *ARQ*—Buster Birch, Deirdre Cartwright, Diane McLoughlin and Steve Lodder—and the contribution made by her wife Jane Reid, formerly a graphic designer, in both photographing the group and creating the publicity and album artwork.

The Alison Rayner Interview

Who would you say influenced your early life—not just in music (include these) but you as a person?

AR: There was a lot of music at home. My uncle, Harry Rayner, was a professional piano player and my dad (his younger brother) loved music and dancing—Frank Sinatra, show songs, that kind of thing. Some of my dad's uncles had a band and he talked about Sunday evenings growing up, with all the family singing songs round the piano. This was all long before television and a time when people made their own entertainment.

My mum loved classical music and the more sophisticated chart stuff including hits of the time like 'Take Five'[14] and she loved the radio. There was often music playing and I remember coming home from school as a child and lying on the floor while she did the ironing with the *Light* or *Third* Programmes (the forerunners to *Radio 2* and *Radio 3*) on, and dance bands or light classical stuff playing.

Dad really encouraged me to play. He gave me his ukulele when I was tiny and showed me some chords, then his Spanish guitar. I would stand at the piano and pick out tunes and he loved it. My older sister Jackie played piano and guitar and brought the first *Beatles* record home. She also listened to

14   Paul Desmond's composition for the Dave Brubeck Quartet.

folk—Joan Baez and Bob Dylan—and the first jazz I ever heard was a British trad jazz record of hers.

My father was a self-made business man with solid working-class roots. He saw himself as an entrepreneur and adopted quite conservative politics which I was always at odds with. But he was warm, charming and confident, believing that working hard and treating people fairly were important.

My mother was from a more middle class, though rather impoverished, Scottish background, with a liberal sensibility. She was into the arts, theatre and books, although she also loved parties and socializing. Mum's background was quite dour. You weren't supposed to have too much fun. She said her mother would make her turn off the Sunday night dance bands on the radio as it wasn't 'appropriate' music for the "Lord's Day".

A huge event in our family was my mother leaving when I was about fourteen. It was unusual in the 1960s for couples to even divorce, so a mother leaving her family was quite unheard of. It had a huge effect on all of us and although over the years I have come to understand some of what happened, it left me with a feeling of sadness inside that has stayed with me all my life, even if mostly well-concealed.

As far as musical influences go, they, of course, were all men. From the pop music of my teenage years to jazz players I discovered in my 20s and 30s. I'm not sure why I thought I could be a musician as there were certainly no female role models for me. Perhaps it didn't dawn on me that women didn't actually play instruments in the music I loved (the trumpet and keyboard player in the fabulous Sly Stone's band—Cynthia Robinson and Rose Stone respectively—were notable exceptions)! I became aware of a few women sax players in the '70s. Kathy Stobart was one, but these were exceptions and I certainly didn't know any women bass players until much later. As I always felt like an outsider in any scenario I was in, maybe it fitted with the view I had of myself and didn't seem so strange.

Why double bass? Can you describe how playing the bass makes you feel/what you like about it /the sounds/anything?

AR: As a teenager I played guitar and sang in bands when I could find people to play with[15]. In the early '70s in Art College, I was drawn to the radical student

15   Not many at the time, if you were a girl in the '60s

politics of the time, later including the women's and gay movements. In 1976 I met some women wanting to form a band. There was a better guitarist than me and we needed a bass player—hence I started playing bass guitar[16]! But it was the first of '*those*' moments when you know something is right for you. As soon as I played it, I was hooked. The bass was my instrument.

The band became *Jam Today* and we were popular within the socialist/feminist/alternative movement of the time, playing squatters and other political benefits, women's festivals and *GLC*[17] events, mostly in the UK, though we also toured in Holland and Germany. Initially we played rock and pop covers, but gradually moved more towards funk, soul and then jazz-influenced music. We started to write our own songs. A strong ethos of the band was a feeling that we must have control. We were opposed to the commercial record industry, which we saw as driven by profit, exploitative of musicians and deeply sexist. We had our own van and PA system and eventually self-released an EP of original songs.

The mid '70s saw a big shift in jazz with the beginnings of what was called 'jazz-rock' at the time, with bands like *Weather Report* and *Return to Forever*. It was exactly the music I had been looking for—challenging and free—but with great grooves and wonderful melodic tunes. I played bass guitar—fretless from 1978—until around 1989, when my great friend, jazz historian and photographer Val Wilmer, told me that her friend Louis Stephenson, wanted to sell his double bass. It felt like another of 'those' moments and I thought this could be where I wanted to go next.

Double bass is a great deal harder to play than bass guitar. There is not just the intonation to get right—a challenge if you've not had classical lessons—but also the sheer physicality of the thing. It took a while to get my hands and fingers strong enough. At first, after one chorus my hand would collapse! For a while, I felt like I was doing battle with it, but we gradually became friends.

For me, playing double bass can be wonderful and it can also feel really hard at times. If it's going well, I feel at one with the instrument, which is a great feeling. I have a beautiful bass and I consider myself very lucky to have such a lovely instrument. I can feel its history and long life. Jazz is such an incredible music as it's full of challenges and surprises. We constantly take risks. So

---

16   Possibly how most bass players start.
17   Greater London Council

sometimes these work—magic—but conversely you can fall flat on your face. You just have to let it go, be in the moment and carry on.

I love the way the bass centers the music and holds the ground between rhythm and harmony. Everyone in the band wants to hear it because it gives them their foundation. I am completely unseated hearing music without some kind of bass in it—can't understand it at all.

I like playing bass in any musical context or genre, but I especially love the way that in jazz, the bass can solo too. It gives a chance for the bass to step forward and for me, improvising a solo is really just a kind of instant composition. But probably my greatest desire is to play notes with a sound. Big, warm, resonant notes that connect with your heart. That's what I'm trying to do.

Have you been involved in education? Do you feel there is still the interest there was a few years ago or is this growing? Do you think education, jazz degrees etc. are making a difference?

I did ten years of teaching in the '90s, then around ten years of popular music examining for an international exam board. I enjoyed teaching but overall, I feel I've done my time. I still enjoy teaching on jazz summer schools which are short courses, and I teach the odd bass lesson if asked.

The development of jazz courses at the conservatoires has made a big difference in bringing younger players and recently many more young women into the music. This in turn has encouraged more diversity with a growing audience of younger people which is essential to keep the music alive. So, it's very good but we also need to value the life experience and wisdom that older musicians can bring to the music. We live in a very youth-oriented society and can neglect to appreciate the value of age in the creative arts.

My own music education was very different from the conservatoire world. I had studied piano until my teens and also did some classical singing and sang with the *BBC Chorus* in my early 20s. But really, once I discovered pop and rock music—that was what I was interested in. I got an electric guitar when I was about fourteen and played in my first band at the girls' school I went to. It was frowned upon by the (classical) music department but we loved it. I was self-taught in popular music until I became interested in jazz and realized I needed to back it up with more theory and harmony.

Being in the Guest Stars in the '80s was a great education as we just listened to records and learned to play the tunes, experimenting with soloing over the changes. There were lots of great musical influences in '80s London too, like free jazz, South African music, lots of Latin players; Salsa and Brazilian. There was so much to hear and be inspired by. In the '90s I went on two years of *Aebersold* jazz summer weeks where I learned masses, including a week of being in a theory class taught by jazz saxophonist and educator Jerry Coker, which was amazing.

Pretty much everything I have learnt has been from listening to music or from other musicians I've been fortunate enough to play with. This includes South Africans, a Ghanaian band I played with, Salsa, folk and Greek fusion, along with so many different aspects of jazz, from Dixieland to free improvised stuff. I suspect there is no finer way to learn.

Have you ever heard someone play and been totally blown away by what you are hearing?

AR: Oh, so very many times! As a child, I heard what was being played in the house. I started to love classical music and was given an EP of Fingal's *Cave*, Mendelssohn's *Hebrides Overture*. I was completely captivated by the romanticism and wild vistas that I could picture. Some of the later composers also really affected me—Sibelius, Vaughan Williams, Elgar.

From around the age of 12 or 13, I was immersed in popular music. I got a transistor radio for my birthday, and listened to Radio Luxembourg under the bedclothes—the station was only on at night. I was first blown away when I heard the Zombies' 'She's Not There' and bought the single the very next day. I bought records whenever I could. I loved the *Beatles, The Who, The Kinks* and other British bands. I discovered the world of Tamla Motown, Jimi Hendrix, Aretha, Stevie Wonder, American soul and funk and so much more besides.

In 1976, I had been playing bass guitar for about two months when I read in the *Melody Maker* about a new US bass player who was releasing his first solo album. This was Jaco Pastorius, who in that same year, recorded with Pat Metheny, Joni Mitchell and joined *Weather Report*. I ordered the record from my local record shop and collected it on release day, went home and put it on my record player. I was completely blown away by it. I had never heard anything like it before. And on bass guitar too! That changed my whole approach to music. I became a huge fan of *Weather Report, Return to Forever* (both bands were such a revolution in the world of bass guitar!), later the *Pat Metheny Group*, then expanded to loads more jazz from other eras.

In 1984, I was touring the East Coast of the US with the *Guest Stars*. We were in New York for a while, so we trawled the jazz clubs and record stores. I found the Bill Evans 'Live at the Village Vanguard' album and heard double bass player Scott LaFaro for the first time—another amazing moment in my life. Quite beautiful.

Charlie Haden is probably my biggest inspiration on double bass. I first saw him play in Berlin in the '80s when we played the *Berlin Jazz Festival* there. He was playing with the *Liberation Orchestra* at the time, but my favourite albums are some of the duo albums he did later. They were so intimate. Also, when he was with Quartet West, who I saw in London. He had such a deep love for melody and the simplest—though most profound—bass playing. One note can say so much.

Are there events in your personal life which have affected your music? Do you think going through major events in life are useful/good for musicians or do they make you close down emotionally?

AR: My music is completely affected by my personal life. Most obviously as a composer, although events and experiences do impact on my bass playing too. I'm not sure how, as an artist, you could be separate from emotions. To me, it's all one and the same. I write music about places and experiences. As I get older, I am writing more music about loss—of relationships, of people close to me. One was a piece I wrote for my father's funeral, which I later developed and recorded with *ARQ* for our first album. I wrote a piece for my mother for our second album. I'd wanted to do that for a long time but it took a while before I could find it. Writing the music feels like my tribute to them. I'm trying to communicate how I felt about them and the effect they had on my life.

In the last three years, I have experienced for the first time the huge impact of the death of a young person through them taking their own life. Firstly, the son of close friends, then two family members—my great-nephew and then my niece. My new album 'Short Stories'[1] has pieces on it that were written for them. It helps me to write—something about trying to accommodate the grief and shock of their sudden loss.

All my music comes from within me and I can't imagine a time where my writing wouldn't be completely personal, whether it's about the loss of someone I loved or being surrounded by the sounds and smells of Kerala or the birdsong in the Australian bush.

Do you feel there is still a harder path for women in jazz music? Is this changing and do you see a future where gender will not be an issue?

AR: This is such a huge topic. When I first started playing professionally (admittedly not in jazz to start with), it was a time where few women played instruments in public. Playing gigs in pubs and colleges, we sometimes attracted attention from men who clearly felt quite threatened by what they saw as an invasion of 'their' space. Being hassled, heckled and generally challenged was not unusual. Guitarist Deirdre Cartwright was told after one rock gig that she must be on drugs, as everyone knows it is impossible for a woman to play so fast!

I suspect that I may have had fewer opportunities in jazz than a man would, but this is only a feeling and it's hard to know what the reality is. In any case, like most other women players, I have just got on with trying to create my own opportunities—and probably kept a lot more control that way! I've also had lots of support and help over the years from other musicians, both men and women.

In any case, the jazz scene revolves a lot around friendship networks. People will often ask people they know well to play. A trumpet player friend, who used to do quite a few pop sessions, said that if she got a call, she knew that she'd only been called because they wanted an all women horn section.

I feel that I have carved out a decent career for myself and am treated with respect these days by my fellow musicians and audience members. Fortunately, these days most men understand that it's not acceptable to behave in an overtly sexist way, even if some still have those feelings inside. Things are definitely changing. I think it's probably seen as a bit cooler now to have women in your band than it was in the past.

Of course, sexism is only one of the thorny issues. Ageism is the other half of this (and of course, you only learn this as you get older)! The two work in tandem, as older women are often seen as irrelevant in our society. Getting less of the overtly sexual or predatory attention as you get older is a great relief, but whereas older men are generally respected in jazz, women can be overlooked.

I long for a day when everyone can be included and appreciated for what they can contribute and gender—or age for that matter—are not considered important enough to be remarked upon.

Do you notice differences in the music scenes (jazz) in the US and elsewhere?

AR: Although I lived in the USA for a year, it was a long time ago (1973-74). I toured there with the *Guest Stars* in 1984. I love New York and have visited a few times since then. But although I have been influenced by a great deal of American—notably Afro-American—music, I don't have any real knowledge of the scene.

How do you feel when you get a review which is not fair or not good?

Luckily, I don't think many jazz reviewers bother to review an album if they don't like it. I think the worst I've had is a couple of reviews which were a little non-committal, but even that is tough. You're thinking, 'they didn't get it'. But of course, in the end, a review is just one person's opinion yet they are also incredibly important in adding weight to publicity and building confidence about the music. Good reviews make you feel good!

You run a label—what inspired you to do this and how do you think it works with being both a musician and label owner? Is it true that there is no money in recordings?

AR: Starting *Blow the Fuse Records* felt like a natural development of our club nights which we had run in a couple of venues, settling down to weekly gigs at the (old) Vortex in Stoke Newington[18], inviting different musicians to play with us each week. We bought one of the first portable DAT recording machines in 1994 and decided to record every gig over a few months. We

---

18   *The Vortex* is one of London's most famous jazz clubs and was based in Stoke Newington before moving to Dalston in 2005.

didn't really understand the technical demands of live recording, so just strung a couple of mics up on the rafters and pressed 'go'! When we listened to the recordings, we thought we had a potential compilation album, so thought we'd better start a record label to release it on. Deirdre (Cartwright) spent hours and hours listening and whittling down to one track from each group or artist. Then we got it edited and mastered and released it. It featured artists such as Ian Shaw, Liane Carroll and John Etheridge, amongst many others.

The record label has subsequently been more of an outlet for our own projects—the *Deirdre Cartwright Group,* our *Blow the Fuse* compilation 'One Night Stands', the *Guest Stars* 'Selected Recordings' and latterly, my three *ARQ* albums. Both Deirdre and I enjoy the production side and of course our efforts these days are a great deal more professional than when we started.

I'm not sure there is any money in anything in jazz really but that isn't why we do it of course. I consider myself incredibly fortunate to have had a life playing music and doing what I want. I've been able to manage fine somehow and made an okay living, sometimes I'm not sure quite how, but I have!

If you could meet your younger self—just about thinking of a career in jazz music, is there any piece of advice you might give her?

AR: Not really. I don't really have any feelings of regret, despite having done many things relatively late in my life. I guess everything happened when it did for a reason and at the right time. Perhaps I would just say, 'have as much confidence as you can and be true to yourself'.

I'm happy that I started my quintet, *ARQ,* when I did. We recorded our first album when I was 60—which on one level seems crazily late to start a solo career—but by then I knew what I wanted to do and how I'd like to do it. I have more confidence now than when I was young and I have my whole life experience to draw on.

Perhaps my only regret is that neither of my parents lived to see the success (modest though it is) of *ARQ.* I think they would have been proud to see the band play, read the reviews and hear us played on the radio. And they would have absolutely loved that I won an *Ivor Novello Award.*

Given a blank canvas, just Alison looking at the world, what would you like to say to people who listen, come to gigs and buy your music?

AR: I'd like you to connect emotionally with the music, for it to mean something to you. I hope you love the tunes, remember them, maybe sing some of them. I hope the music helps you in some way—whether that is to remind you of places or experiences, picture things in your imagination, grieve for someone you've lost or just feel uplifted.

Shirley Smart

"Listen to your heart and your instincts. There will be moments, periods of self-doubt. Accept it and work through it. Keep working—even without a deadline—keep writing, keep notes, make recordings and let projects formulate organically over time. Choose your band-mates and colleagues carefully—work with people who support you, that you trust and who allow you to be yourself."

Shirley Smart is a cellist who trained under Raphael Wallfisch at the *Guildhall School of Music* in London and Janos Starker in Paris before relocating to Jerusalem where she stayed for ten years studying and performing with musicians steeped in the traditions of Turkey, North Africa and the Middle East. She brings her combination of Eastern influenced music and improvisational skills to her music. Her collaborations include those with Maya Youssef, Gilad Atzmon, James Arben and Robert Mitchell. She has played with Yo Yo Ma, Yazid Fentazi, Neil Cowley and many more. Shirley also leads her own trio, the Shirley Smart Trio, and a band called Melange. Shirley is one of the UK's most creative, versatile and recognized 'cellists. She teaches at the *Royal College of Music* and is a visiting tutor for the Youth Jazz Collective. In this interview Shirley discussed the pros and cons of jazz education, jazz in Jerusalem, the dangers of tokenism and how venues in the UK might make musicians a little more welcome.

The Shirley Smart Interview

Who would you say influenced your early life—not just in music but you as a person?

SSm: Very early on, I would say my 'cello teacher, who was a hilarious character by the name of Phil. He was a Yorkshire-man, and a very lively and charismatic person, who taught me from the age of 10-18. I was never that easily influenced as a child—I was quite strong-willed and was mostly interested in 'cellos!

Why the 'cello—Can you describe how playing the 'cello makes you feel, what you like about it?

SSm: I love the register of the 'cello especially—I have a contralto voice and I generally prefer the middle/lower ranges of voices as well. There's also the timbre of the instrument—the sound quality that I love. Of course, it is a very physical instrument and I do really love the feeling of being connected to it when you draw the bow across the string.

You have been involved in education and teaching. How do you feel about young people and jazz? Do you feel there is still the interest there was a few years ago or is this growing? Do you think education—jazz degrees etc. are making a difference?

SSm: I have mixed feelings about institutionalized jazz courses. It's great that jazz is recognized at tertiary level, but I think there is a risk of developing cliques and a set mentality about what jazz can be. But having access to recording facilities, great teachers and a peer group with shared interests is of great value. One often sees bands on the professional scene who have worked together since college and have a really tightly knit connection because of that. This does have two sides, though—as I said, it can run the risk of developing very clear 'in-groups' and 'out-groups'. Institutions are a great help in access to industry contacts and so forth however.

That being said, I think musicians with something to say will find their path regardless—and there are many people on the scene who also bear that out. I think there is certainly interest among young people—although my fear in the UK is that music education generally is declining in primary and secondary schools, so people are not getting the same exposure early on. This will have a significant effect in five or ten years. Having said that, organizations such as the *National Youth Jazz Collective*, the *National Youth Jazz* orchestra and Tomorrow's Warriors keep a strong outlet and community available to younger musicians and are thriving. There are so many really interesting and strong young players on the scene—both male and female—that I think jazz is pretty safe for a bit.

On your years in the Middle East—what made you decide to go and study/work there? What is the music scene like there and jazz in particular? Did the music you found there influence your playing or ideas? What made you decide to come back to the UK?

SSm: Well, I spent 10 years in Jerusalem—which was not something I ever really intended to do, but it was totally a life changer! I went on an exchange scholarship, ostensibly for a year—and mostly as the result of an accidental conversation with someone in Canada over a snooker table, with a fair amount of red wine involved! I was thinking of going somewhere to study further but was unsure where, and this conversation persuaded me to explore the possibility of Jerusalem. It just looked interesting—and it was.

The musical scene is small but very rich, as the amount of different musical traditions that are indigenous to the region and whose histories overlap in Jerusalem is enormous. All the various communities who have immigrated to Israel have bought their respective traditions with them, as well as the Palestinian folk traditions and Arabic/Turkish traditions that are there. I became involved with almost all of them, as I played with both Jewish and Arabic, Israeli and Palestinian musicians while I was there and learned so much from all of them.

There is also a very small, but fertile and intense jazz scene; and the fluidity with the regional traditions is fascinating. I think it is very different to the UK where those regional traditions would be treated more as 'world music'—a very problematic term, but for the moment I'll use it as it has, for better or worse, shaped the way that certain music is viewed and conceived, which is interesting in itself. Actually, I am writing a PhD which will contain some exploration of this. In Jerusalem, I think the notion of 'world music' is redundant, as they are simply local traditions. I think it very much changes the dynamic of the relationship between the fields. Anyway, there was a wonderful centre called the *International Centre for Creative Music*, run by a saxophonist called Arnie Lawrence, where many of the jazz musicians used to meet for workshops and jam sessions. We also used to hang out in a soup bar called the *Marakiya*, where sometimes musicians like Avishai Cohen and Omer Avital would drop in when they were in Israel. It was very lively and dynamic.

This period absolutely changed my musical direction and still is central to the way I approach writing my own music as I cannot separate the influence of the North African/Turkish and Arabic music that I played and the jazz.

Are there other events in your personal life which have affected your music? Do you think going through major events in life are useful/ good for musicians or do they make you close down emotionally?

SSm: I think this is very variable according to the individual. Major trauma can be healed by music, or it can help one focus, or it may be that it can cause someone to stop playing for a period of time. I don't think there's any one rule about that.

Do you feel there is a harder path for women in jazz music? Is this changing and do you see a future where gender will not be an issue?

SSm: This is a very interesting question, and perhaps one that requires different answers in different places. In the UK, I think the situation has certainly improved. I see firstly a lot of really excellent female instrumentalists on the scene now and secondly a really changed mentality among many younger male musicians. This is a very healthy development and one that I really think should be acknowledged.

At the same time, some old attitudes still linger on, sadly, and I think across Europe, if one looks at the line-ups of festivals, it is still very male dominated. I know that a lot of festivals have signed up to the Keychange Pledge[19] to make their line-ups 50/50 by 2022. This is a positive sign, although I do wonder what is so difficult about just doing it now- there's not exactly a shortage of players.

There's been many initiatives to tackle gender imbalance which is great—but I do sometimes worry that such things can result in tokenism, which isn't helpful at all. It feels to me like it is far more complicated that it should be,

---

19   *Keychange* is a pioneering international initiative which empowers women to transform the future of music. Over 150 festivals around the world have signed up to the Keychange pledge of aiming for a 50:50 gender balanced line-up by 2022.

and what needs to change is the mentalities that perpetuate gender stereotypes or negative ideas toward women in jazz. It's just a bit silly.

I think it will remain an issue for a while yet but I do see change. So, I am hopeful but it is a bit slow.

Also, to be honest, I have had more prejudicial reactions because of the instrument, rather than being female—which also seems to generate a reaction for some reason. Fortunately, though, I think people are getting used to the idea of 'cellos as well. Again, it's not that complicated!

It can be a double edged sword, as the 'cello is a 'novelty' so it stands out as being a bit different, but at the same time some promoters say things like, 'oh, our audiences want a straight ahead line-up', despite the fact that I can offer a 'straight ahead' set. But it's fine, I have plenty of performance opportunities and I have had a very positive response to my first album 'Long Story Short' (33 Xtreme 2019), with a UK tour next year, and several festival performances this year and next, so open-minded people are definitely out there!

Do you notice differences in the music scenes in the UK and elsewhere, even in the UK itself?

SSm: I spoke before about the differences between the scene in Jerusalem and the UK. One thing that is distinctly different in Europe, for example, though is hospitality. I realize that many venues in the UK function on a shoe-string but sometimes it is a bit galling not to be offered a hot meal when you have driven three or four hours to get to a location.

I know you play at both large venues and smaller ones—how do these differ in atmosphere, reaction and so on? Do you have a preference?

SSm: I don't mind either—so long as the sound system is good and the audience are listening to the music. Smaller venues have a lovely immediacy and intimacy about them and one can almost speak to individual people. Larger venues can sometimes be more difficult to create that in, but then also the character of the performance might well be very different. For example, when I play in the band of Mulatu Astatke, it is usually fairly large venues but it is an 8-piece band. We have a huge sound system and the music is trance-inducing and invites people to dance. With my own trio, it is a different type of thing and a different kind of stage is more suitable.

If you could meet your younger self—just about thinking of a career in jazz music, 'cello in hand, is there any piece of advice you might give her?

SSm: Do not give up, and don't take any notice whatsoever of people who tell you, you cannot, or should not want to play jazz on the 'cello. Listen to your heart and your instincts. There will be moments, periods of self-doubt. Accept it and work through it. Keep working—even without a deadline—keep writing, keep notes, make recordings and let projects formulate organically over time. Choose your band-mates and colleagues carefully—work with people who support you, that you trust and who allow you to be yourself. Stand your ground with others. Take responsibility for your own stuff. Be wary of insincerity, and people who only talk to you if you're useful to them. Know who your real friends are. Have fun!

Mimi Fox

"Music is precious to me and the ability to share it is a great gift that I never take for granted."

"When I was a young musician playing with a funk band, a respected guitarist came to the show and said to me: "You play pretty good rhythm Mimi but you shouldn't try to solo, girls just can't do this."

Mimi Fox is one of the most influential guitar players of the present day. She has won *Downbeat Magazine International Critics Poll* six times and her playing is consistently praised for being of the highest quality. She has performed with many of jazz's luminaries including David Sanchez, Branford Marsalis, Charlie Byrd, Billy Hart, Terri Lyne Carrington and many more. Her recordings encompass styles which, though rooted firmly in jazz, venture into other music genres. She plays folk, classical, jazz and popular music, including her own compositions and a healthy dose of improvisation. Her ability to master any genre makes her a diverse and wide-reaching player. Mimi's schedule is grueling but she still finds time for projects she feels strongly enough about, one of which, I am pleased to say, was giving me an interview for the book. Here, Mimi discusses being moved to tears by Julian Bream's playing and the life-changing effect of John Coltrane, coming through cancer, the difficulties in erasing misogyny and sexism, and much more.

The Mimi Fox Interview

Who would you say influenced your early life—not just musically but you as a person?

MF: My mother was a huge musical influence because she loved jazz and classical music. She exposed me to everything from Gershwin and Billie Holiday to Shostakovich and Bach. She was also a singer and songwriter and helped me construct some of my first songs. When I was fourteen, I had a music teacher who changed my life because of her encouragement and boundless enthusiasm for music. Her name was Joyce Boguski. The other big influences on me personally were my grandfather who had endured tremendous adversity to come to the United States from Russia as a 14-year-old, and all the great leaders and artists involved in the Civil Rights movement including Dr. Martin Luther King Jr., Harry Belafonte, Lena Horne, and Mahalia Jackson. As a teenager, the great leaders of the women's movement including Gloria Steinem, Margaret Sloan-Hunter and Flo Kennedy had a big impact on me.

Why guitar? Can you describe how playing the guitar makes you feel, what you like about it?

MF: I love everything about the guitar; the sound of the instrument; the feel of it resonating against my body; the immediacy of touching the strings with my fingers to create music. I love drums and bass and play both of these instruments as well. I also love 'cello, bassoon, and pretty much all instruments, but the guitar will always be my deepest musical connection. When I started playing at age ten, I knew that I would devote my life to music and to this majestic instrument.

You have been involved in education. How do you feel about young people and jazz? Do you feel there is still the interest there was a few years ago and is this growing? Do you think education—jazz degrees are making a difference?

MF: Jazz music continues to be a deeply inspiring/compelling art form for people of all ages. I see this is a player when on tour and I see it as an educator. I believe it continues to grow and thrive. Degrees in jazz can be helpful but the best lessons I have had are on the band stand with great players.

Have you ever heard someone play and been totally blown away by what you are hearing?

MF: When I was twelve, I heard the great classical guitarist/lutist Julian Bream in concert and found his music so moving that I started sobbing. At eighteen, I heard McCoy Tyner in concert and that was another deeply moving experience. The most compelling early musical experience was hearing John Coltrane play 'Naima'. I was fourteen at the time and this was a life changing experience for me. The beauty, depth, passion, and eloquence of his playing reached me on a deep level.

I know you have come through cancer—are you willing to describe how this affected you and whether music helped at the time, during recovery or now?

MF: As a composer and musician, I experience life through my ears most profoundly. Therefore, everything that happens to me and around me has an impact and is then filtered through me. Going through cancer was a terrifying, humbling, and ultimately deeply transformative experience. My most recent album, 'This Bird Still Flies'[20] is a testament to resilience and certainly having music as a means to come to grips with my experience was a blessing. But I write and play music through all the ups and downs of life. Not because of the ups and downs, but because this is what I do. This is how I experience life.

Are there other events in your personal life which have affected your music? Do you think going through major events in life are useful/ good for musicians or do they make you close down emotionally?

MF: I try not to ever close down emotionally because this is not good on

---

20   Origin Records 2019

either a personal or musical level. As an artist, I need to stay open so I can experience the full range of life-good and bad.

Do you feel there is still a harder path for women in jazz music? Is this changing and do you see a future where gender will not be an issue?

MF: The fact that you (or anyone) has to ask this question shows that it is still, unfortunately, relevant. Yes, it is still harder for women. Sexism and misogyny are woven so deeply into our culture that it will take a long time to eradicate. I think things are changing but not as fast as most of us would wish. I hope I live to see a future where gender will not be an issue but I wouldn't want to bet on it. When I was a young musician playing with a funk band, a respected guitarist came to the show and said to me: "You play pretty good rhythm Mimi but you shouldn't try to solo. Girls just can't do this." I was very angry at the time, of course. However, this just made me practice harder and I was able to let go of the negativity this man evinced. Other young women might not have had my persistence. Ultimately, I began to ignore these types of comments completely and not to personalize them. I came to understand these comments were a reflection of the person making them and had nothing to do with me. Worse than these comments however, was the locker-room sleaziness of hanging out with musicians during breaks or after shows and having to fend off both unwanted advances and vulgar or sexist jokes. I started bringing buddies to jam sessions and shows so as to have strength in numbers and this helped.

Do you notice differences in the music scenes (jazz in particular) in the US and elsewhere, even in the US itself?

MF: There are great jazz musicians the world over.

How is the scene in the US?

MF: It goes through ups and downs, but I believe it is durable.

If you could meet your younger self—just about thinking of a career in jazz music, guitar in hand, is there any piece of advice you might give her?

MF: I would give her loads of love and try to instill self-confidence in her. I would tell her that she doesn't have to push herself quite so hard.

Given a blank canvas, just Mimi looking at the world, what would you like to say to people who listen, come to gigs and buy your music?

MF: I would thank everyone for listening to my music and tell them that I play to express everything in my heart, mind and soul. I hope they can feel that I give 1,000% to every show; every song, every note. Music is precious to me and the ability to share it is a great gift that I never take for granted.

♭ ♭ ♭

Brandee Younger

"I think music totally relates to society. All art relates to society, one way or another. I'm actually feeling good about music right now. I feel fortunate to have such great players right underneath my nose. There's never a boring moment.

Brandee Younger is an American harpist. She leads her own quartet and performs both as a solo artist and in collaboration with other musicians such as Pharoah Sanders, Jack DeJohnette, Charlie Haden, Ryan Leslie, John Legend, Drake and Ravi Coltrane. Brandee is an educator, concert curator and recording artist. She is a prolific musical performer and has featured as a soloist with *The Harlem Chamber Players* and the *Hartford Symphony Orchestra,* the *Waterbury Symphony* and many other classical ensembles. She self-manages and teaches, maintaining a full schedule as a private instructor and teacher at *Greenwich House Music School* in New York City as well as lecturing at many other established institutions in the UK, Europe and the US. She is Director-at-Large of the *American Harp Society, Inc.* and in 2016 Brandee curated the weekly *Harp on Park* lunchtime concert series which highlighted the diversity of the harp and the contemporary importance of an ancient instrument. In 2019 she curated *Her Song*, highlighting the works of women composers for *Arts Brookfield.* She has been included in several important books.

In this interview, Brandee talks of music and society, the positive hope of the future and men complaining about women getting more work in music, the value of mentors and much more.

The Brandee Younger interview

Who would you say influenced your early life—not just in music but you as a person?

BY: I think that aside from my parents, of whom I am an equal 50/50 split of each, my maternal grandmother had the most influence on me as a person. Her strength, perseverance and entrepreneurial qualities really impacted me.

Why the harp? Can you describe how playing the harp makes you feel/what you like about it /the sounds/anything?

BY: The harp was introduced to me when I was a pre-teen. It was a very practical decision at the time between my parents and myself, as they learned that my chances of receiving a scholarship would be increased with an 'endangered' instrument. Playing it, for me, is both scary and comforting at the same time. The technical act of playing it is the scary part, and the sound that it produces is the comforting part. People always say that the harp has healing qualities and it really, truly does.

You have been involved in education at colleges and universities. How do you feel about young people and jazz? Do you feel there is still the interest there was a few years ago or is this growing?

BY: I think that there is still interest. More than anything, however, I'm noticing students wanting to just play 'music' and to blur the lines between genres.

Do you think jazz degrees are making a difference?

BY: Degree or no degree, I think it's important for players to have technical facility on their instruments before branching out into the professional world. I believe that this can be achieved with or without a formal degree.

Have you ever heard someone play and been totally blown away by what you are hearing? Can you explain what it is about someone's playing which catches your attention?

BY: Definitely the first time I heard Pharoah Sanders live. And to piggyback off your last question, what I heard that night was nothing that school could ever teach. Without question, it was the spirit behind the playing that enraptured me. I'm not moved so much by 'notey' playing, but by 'feely' playing (smile).

Following on from this, when you curate concerts, what do you look for in performers? Do you have a programme or aim in mind or how does this work?

BY: I try to look at genre/style diversity first. If I don't do this, I'd probably end up curating a bunch of the same kind of music. So I make an effort to cover multiple bases to the best of my ability. That is probably one of the greatest joys of being based in NYC, as we have so many wonderful musical options.

I know you play classical and other genres as well as jazz music. Can you say what is it about jazz which is appealing for you? How do you feel your music fits with the ever- changing modern ideas of music?

BY: Yes, all of my formal training is in classical music. I knew early on that I wanted to do something more, and over the years realized that I wanted to be able to express myself more. My music is a smash-up of different styles, so, I suppose that is the way that it fits with the ever-changing modern ideas of music. Also, it doesn't hurt that I play an odd instrument, too.

Are there events in your life which have affected your music? Do you think going through major events or seeing events happen around us are useful/good for musicians or do they make you close down emotionally?

BY: I think that for many, the climate around us affects our output (whether in a good or bad way). I do think that it's good as it fosters creativity. The first time that I felt compelled to compose after something that happened, was when Trayvon Martin[21] was murdered. It was the first time that a composition come to me without effort.

Do you feel there is still a harder path for women in jazz/music? Is this changing and do you see a future where gender will not be an issue?

BY: Sure. There are way more men in the music than women. Of course, at this moment, I do hear lots of men complain or comment on women getting more work as a result of the *#MeToo* movement but we all know gender is a major issue in the workforce, period. I do see a future where gender won't be so much of an issue. We're on our way.

How is the scene in the US? Is it secure, growing, shrinking?

BY: I was afraid that it was shrinking, but then I just began to notice a shift. So, I believe that it is growing, just sort of in a different direction.

If you could meet your younger self—just about thinking of a career in jazz music, harp in hand, is there any piece of advice you might give her?

BY: The advice I'd give little Brandee is to not worry about what others think and do what you want (or what you think you want). I would've done it much sooner—and slightly more assertively, too.

Given a blank canvas, just Brandee looking at the world, what would you like to say to people who listen, come to gigs and buy your music?

BY: Thank You! Gratitude!

I understand you self-manage and have always done this. Is this still the same and why do you self-manage?

---

21   Trayvon Benjamin Martin was a 17-year-old African-American teenager from Miami Gardens, Florida, who was fatally shot in Sanford, Florida by George Zimmerman in 2012 on his way back from a convenience store. Zimmerman was a member of the community watch and on spotting Trayvon, reported him to the police. A few minutes later after an altercation, Zimmerman shot Trayvon in the chest, fatally wounding him. Though Zimmerman was charged and tried, he was acquitted of second-degree murder and manslaughter. Initially, the police had cited the state's stand your ground laws as the reason for not arresting Zimmerman and arrested him only after public outcry.

BY: I am just beginning to work with management now. And I have self-managed all of these years because nobody would manage me! Totally out of necessity.

For the future, how do you see music and society? There is a saying that jazz music in particular reflects society. Would you agree with this or do you think music is unrelated to society?

BY: I think music totally relates to society. All art relates to society, one way or another. I'm actually feeling good about music right now. I feel fortunate to have such great players right underneath my nose. There's never a boring moment.

Is there anything else you might want to add?

BY: I think it's important to mention not just the state of music, but the state of players and their music 'upbringing'. I'm a strong advocate of mentoring and that's the one thing I feel is not being valued as it should. Every person needs a mentor, and needs to help others. I guess that's why I feel so fulfilled within my 'tribe' as folks are saying now. I have elders that give me guidance and my peers and I help each other out and pull each other up, and we help those in need. It's this cyclical process of pulling others along while being pulled. That needs to grow.

Ginetta Vendetta

"... to be able to bring my musical ideas to fruition with amazing musicians and hear them played, then recorded and sent out into the world is a feeling unlike any other."

"You must have the hide of an alligator, the heart of a lion and the perseverance of a tortoise to last and succeed in this business of music."

Ginetta Minichiello, *aka* Ginetta Vendetta is a trumpet player, vocalist, composer and bandleader. She was born in Italy and came to the US as a baby. She began learning trumpet when she was just eight years old and knew it was right for her. She studied at North Texas State University and plays most styles of music from classical, funk and pop to blues and jazz. Her teachers have included Spanky Davis, Ted Curson and Allan Colin as well as several others. She has played with Charles Neville, Jimmy Buffet, Albert Collins and many other musicians and received the *Ascaplus Award* for song writing and the legendary *Black Music Award*. After 9/11, Ginetta was awarded the *Music Liberty Initiative for New York City* musicians. The story goes that Ginetta originally wanted to learn the trombone but her small stature and short arms meant she found the trumpet suited her better. She has been called a powerhouse for her energy and talent and she has played across the world, held residencies on cruise ships and clubs, played festivals. Her music has been in nine Grammy nomination categories. Ginetta has recorded five CDs and leads her trio, Ginetta's Vendetta, at many events. Her aim is to achieve 'Peace through Music'.

In her interview, Ginetta talks about the effect of gender fluidity, gratitude, working in different countries of the world, advice to her younger self-regarding studying and lots more.

The Ginetta Vendetta Interview

Can you tell me about your influences early in my life, not just in music, but as a person?

GV: I would have to say my father, who is a jazz buff, was one of the major influences in my early life and in encouraging me to play the trumpet. My first choice, however, was the trombone, but my wonderful music teacher Mr. Cirocillo (another major influence through grade school) said that my arms were too short! So, I chose trumpet and was the first chair all through grammar school. As time goes on, I also realize how much my beautiful and stylish mother was a major influence on me with her cool shades, head scarves and bangles, plus her elegant outfits and non-conformist style. She always looked like a movie star when she dressed up to go to one of the many parties my parents frequented and often hosted!

My early musical influences were the guys Pop would always call me downstairs to see on the TV: Dizzy Gillespie, Louis Armstrong, Maynard Ferguson (who I had the honor of meeting at a music camp when I was young) or whatever other trumpeter was on TV at the time. I listened to Clifford Brown all the time in the beginning trying to emulate his beauty of tone and fat as well as lots of Ella Fitzgerald and Sarah Vaughan. Also, lots of R& B stars: Chaka Khan, *Earth, Wind and Fire*, Aretha Franklin and others. To augment my musical education Pop started taking me to jazz clubs when I was eleven or twelve on the most famous jazz block in NYC—52nd Street! There was Eddie Condon's, Jimmy Ryan's, *The Half Note* and more. There I met my first professional teacher, Ted Curson, with whom I studied weekly for about two years. I also got to meet Dizzy Gillespie, Roy 'Little Jazz' Eldridge and another amazing trumpeter Spanky Davis who I also studied with.

Why the trumpet? Can you describe how playing it makes you feel, what you like about it, the sound, anything!?

GV: As I previously explained the trumpet was my second choice, but after playing it for a while, I realized that it suited me and my leadership personality perfectly. Did I acquire the attributes of the trumpet: bossy, noticeable, out-front, not shy, but also subtle, beautiful, hard-hitting, brassy, fun and lively? Or did the trumpet—the driving instrument behind every big band, Latin, jazz or funk—fit me perfectly from the start? When I'm playing *well* it makes me feel whole. Plus, it is the closest to heaven that mere mortals will ever get, especially when I'm creating and playing with other musical masters! I love the tone of the horn when it's played correctly, with its big, fat sound and gorgeous sonorous tones in the middle and low registers and its clarion-like sound in the upper ones. It is a sacred instrument thousands of years old and played by archangel Gabriel. What more can I say? A veritable 'Queen of Instruments'. It is also the hardest to play as it incorporates every part of your face and body.

How do you feel about young people and jazz? Is there still an interest in it and is it growing? Do you think the education/jazz degrees are making a difference?

GV: I feel that without these young people continuing the legacy of jazz, it would be a lost art. In my travels and performances, I always say, 'America's greatest export is jazz' and that depends on it being carried on by the next generation of 'Young Lions' or in this case 'Lionesses' of jazz. I believe the interest has not waned but rather the publicity has. In the past, jazz was the pop music of the day. Now, due to lack of radio stations, finances, publicity and so on jazz has been relegated to the background. We need more emphasis on it during the endless music shows that are on T.V. Let's put the musicians front and center, or at least show them a few times during various variety/reality programs. Why not televise the jazz portion of the *Grammys* as well, instead of the mind-numbing lip-synching performances overwhelmed with dancers? Why shouldn't those amazing musicians, vocalists and composers have a moment in the spotlight like the others? Let's proclaim from television and stage the importance of creating, maintaining, and supporting this classic art form that *is* an American treasure by uplifting musically, socially and financially the jazz musician!

As far as degrees go, they might help on paper but nothing can substitute real-life experience—though the killer musicians coming out of these universities most definitely have added advantages with their sight-reading, theory, composition and more.

However, I feel it's important not to sacrifice feeling and/or beauty of tone with over-blowing on solos and too much 'cerebral' playing. As one of the greats said (was it Clark Terry?) 'What you don't play is as important as what you do play' and that is why I believe in aural space so the music can breathe.

In your tours through other countries, what is the music scene like there? Jazz In particular? Did the music you found there influence your playing or ideas on playing?

Over the years I have had the pleasure of traveling through many countries and playing with the musicians of those countries. I always say that America and NYC in particular does *not* have the best musicians in the world. Yes, perhaps the best *congregate* here in town... But in my travels, I have been blessed to play with some of the best musicians in each country I play in and the jazz scenes are steady and thriving, though it might be smaller depending on the size of the country.

In Beirut, I had the pleasure of playing with the top piano players (Hani & Arthur, drummer Walid and bass player Abooud). These musicians rivalled any and all in the world with their musicality, professionalism and jazz chops. The goes same for my steady band in Mexico out of Guadalajara; Wille Z. on keys, Jonny X. on bass and Archie S. on drums. Amazing musicians all! Ditto for my band in Jamaica—the phenomenal *Desi Jones Trio*. Not to mention all the superlative musicians I've met whenever I play in the Midwest or Canada, the Cayman Islands, Russia, Eastern Europe or anywhere in the world. Jazz is alive and well internationally thanks to these amazing musicians, both men and women. In my early career I toured much through South America, Puerto Rico and the Caribbean, so the music of those Islands (calypso, merengue and salsa) infused many of my original tunes from my first CD: 'La Dolce Vita'. The beautiful music of the Middle East also inspired me to open my ears to alternate tones and pitches and gave me a sense of musical possibility.

Are there events in your personal life that have affected your music? Do you think going through major events in life are useful/good for musicians or do they make you close down emotionally?

GV: Of course, there have been major events that have affected me adversely. Love affairs gone awry, tour cancellations, my mother's passing, mouth injuries, etc. but to rise above this is what makes the mark of a true and dedicated professional musician. Not to give up, go 'off the rails' or continually dwell on the negativity is what forges a diamond in both character and musicality! During a mouth injury last summer, I found that I could actually carry the whole gig vocally, without my horn. That was a liberating discovery for me at the time, but playing is my true calling and passion and I would never want to be without the ability to do so. My Mom used to say, 'there will always be someone better than you' which served to light a fire in me to be the best at what I do, regardless of life's opportunities disguised as 'obstacles'. I believe going through life's events, both good and bad, are what create a 'seasoned' musician; one who is able to express their emotions through their chosen instrument, voice included, which is so important when singing and allowing others to feel that emotion. To transport people to another place, uplifting them is what real talent is. I do not close down emotionally—at least not while trying to create and perform—because leaving oneself open to those emotions is what channels great art. Many of my original tunes have come from a place of despair and/or sadness.

Do you feel there is still a harder path for women in jazz music? Is this changing and do you see a future where gender is not an issue?

GV: When I was coming up, in NYC, in the late 80's, early 90's there were very few female musicians and we all knew each other. I was often the only woman in an all-male ensemble whether it was Latin, funk, big band, blues or a show band. The common phrase was always, 'you play great for a girl' and I would always reply, 'I play great, period!' I was most definitely one of the female musical pioneers in the early days, both as a trumpet player, then a bandleader (since 1993!); but the real female trailblazer of the trumpet was the amazing Laurie Frink, a fabulous player, teacher and mentor to many. As for the question is it *currently* a harder path for women—I would have to say not nearly as bad now, almost thirty-five years later. I do see that in the future gender will not be an issue since gender fluidity as a whole has started to permeate the public consciousness.

You play both large venues and smaller ones- how does this differ in atmosphere, reaction and so on. Do you have a preference?

GV: I have been blessed to play some very large concert halls and stages as well as being tucked into a corner of tiny restaurants. The difference is that in the smaller venues, you are n*ot* the center of attention and are merely providing ambiance for the venue while mostly being ignored. On the bigger stages, *you* are the center of attention and your musicality and showmanship is vastly appreciated and really, who doesn't prefer that? But, as a professional bandleader here in NYC for over twenty-five years it is my responsibility to keep us working in between festival and tour appearances, regardless of venue size. When you become ungrateful and bitter about situations the music suffers. I am always happy to be playing and getting paid for it, which is what I was born to do. Sometimes if the guys remark on it, I will tell them, 'at least you're not washing dishes or waiting tables.' When you bring joy to your playing, regardless of venue size people notice and appreciate your talents and efforts. To me that is the whole idea of being a musician—to spread joy and peace through music.

You have been called a 'triple-threat female powerhouse' as you play, sing and compose, how do you feel about that and how does it feel if you ever somehow don't get through to someone, for example, if you get a poor review?

GV: I feel empowered by my triple threat status and very happy to be able to both play and sing as well as compose and set my emotions and experiences to music. When I'm on a long gig or have double and triple gigs in a day or night, or when I'm on a particularly grueling tour I feel very grateful to be able to rest my chops and sing and then rest my voice and play. It is a win-win situation and very helpful that I am well versed in both. Also, to be able to bring my musical ideas to fruition with amazing musicians and hear them played, then recorded and sent out into the world is a feeling unlike any other. As far as any negative press (which I haven't gotten yet, give thanks!) I would try to ignore it just as I have ignored negative people throughout my entire career. I often tell people that you must have the hide of an alligator, the heart of a lion and the perseverance of a tortoise to last and succeed in this business of music. In other words, I am impervious to naysayers and try to distance myself from any negativity which I do not encounter very often!

If you could meet your younger self, just thinking of a career in Jazz Music, Horn in hand, is there any piece of advice you would give her?

GV: 'Study medicine' ha ha!! I have only one regret in life which is pretty amazing and that is not finishing my musical studies at the *N.T.S.U.* one of the preeminent music schools in the country back in the day. I would tell my younger self to, *'please* study, practice, listen to those ear training and theory teachers, (which I thought were so boring at the time). Go to class, do your musical due diligence and graduate so you will be adequately prepared to go out into the music world.' As it happened, I only lasted a year at that school and started playing professionally immediately after moving in to NYC. At the age of seventeen. I practiced up to six hours a day because my livelihood depended on it. I feel, however that I would have been better equipped to get higher paying gigs with jazz orchestras, Broadway shows, touring companies etc. if my sight reading and musical acumen had been up to par. As it happened, I played so many different types of music that in the long run I became even more proficient and a seasoned professional after all through actual experience.

Given a Blank canvas, just you (Ginetta) looking at the listening and interested world, what would you like to say to people who listen, come

to your gigs and buy your music?

GV: 'Thank you!' That is what I would say first and foremost. 'Thank you for listening and supporting me by buying my CDs and coming to my shows.' I would also love to tell them how very important and integral to life music is. How we as musicians, need to be supported, encouraged, lauded and respected in this world with many more financial opportunities for us to create and get paid for it a living comfortable wage. This road is not an easy one and I often say that being a musician is like taking a vow to the church, one of poverty, abstinence and discipline (at first) where all you do, know, live and breathe is music. As the wonderful bass player, Mickey Bass, once told me decades ago: 'You take care of music and it will take care of you.'

Taeko Kunishima

"I found the piano can express the music very well by creating dynamics, legato melodic lines, and percussionist staccato. You can also reach into the instrument to play on the strings, on the wood, and metal surfaces to create different timbres."

Taeko Kunishima is a jazz pianist who switched from classical to jazz after listening to Miles Davis. She moved to London and incorporates traditional Japanese music into her repertoire, frequently composing for and collaborating with *shakuhachi*[22] and *shamisen*[23]. She has worked with musicians including Clive Bell and David Bower and she has played festivals including the *London Jazz Festival* and the *Isle of Wight Festival* as well as performing at venues such as *The Vortex* jazz club. Taeko has also performed live works for radio. Here she discusses music in Japan, the joys of a well-tempered piano and the reality of being a jazz musician.

---

22   The *shakuhachi* is a Japanese wooden, end blown flute.

23   The *shamisen* is a three-stringed traditional Japanese musical instrument, played with a plectrum called *bachi* (also called *samisen* or *sangen*).

The Taeko Kunishima Interview

SS Who would you say influenced your early life, not just in music but you as a person?

TK: I was influenced by my neighbour's kids, who were about my age, my mother, my brother and in some ways, my father who died when I was only two years old. When I was about five years old, I had dreams about him sometimes and I remember looking for him when I was toddler. Obviously, he didn't teach me music or about life, there was only his violin, the picture of Rodin's 'Thinker', his books and his study desk. I picked up his books to read and I loved to listen to classical music.

Can you tell me what drew you to jazz?

TK: I heard Miles Davis's modal jazz on the radio when I was studying classical music… It could have been 'Kind of Blue'… I felt like I was out in the universe. It sounded very mystical. I started to listen to Miles Davis, Keith Jarrett and Chick Corea. At the same time, I was listening to modern classical composers including Toru Takemitsu, Schoenberg, and impressionist classical composers, such as Debussy, Ravel and Satie.

Why piano—Can you describe how playing the piano makes you feel, what you like about it, the sounds?

TK: The piano is the ideal instrument for writing music, as well as learning chords and scales.

The twelve notes per octave of the standard keyboard are tuned in a way that it is possible to play music in major or minor keys, so you can play the tunes easily. Playing a well-tempered piano, makes it relatively easier to learn chords and scales than on other instruments. I found the piano can express the music very well by creating dynamics, legato melodic lines, and percussionist staccato.

You can also reach into the instrument to play on the strings, on the wood, and metal surfaces to create different timbres.

What is the music scene like in Japan in particular?

TK: American mainstream jazz describes the overall jazz scene in Japan. Free jazz and experimental jazz musicians play in small jazz venues. Most jazz fans are males who are interested in young female musicians; quite often young female vocalists especially.

They don't necessarily appreciate their music but go for their physical appearance. That's the reality of the Japanese jazz scene.

I know you played at the London jazz festival and also at the smaller venues like the Vortex in Dalston. How do you find the difference playing large and small events? Do you have a preference?

TK: I prefer small venues with a very well-tuned grand piano. Unfortunately, there are lots of small venues in UK which haven't even got pianos. If we have an audience who are good listeners and can relate to my original music, we really enjoy performing, but if we are not sure, then we feel more nervous and can't enjoy performing.

You collaborate with other instrumentalists, particularly those playing Japanese instrument like the shakuhach₁ and shamisen₂. Does this work well? How do these instruments lend themselves to playing your arrangements?

TK: I write *shamisen* and *shakuhachi* parts to suit my requirements for my compositions. In the solo parts, they improvise with the flavours of my compositions. And I am Japanese: therefore, Japanese instruments give the full expression which defines my musical identity.

Are there events in your life which have affected your music? Do you think going through major events in life is a good thing for musicians or do they make you close down emotionally?

TK: I believe studying music can help in understanding the basic knowledge of music to enable playing the instruments and writing music. But if you want to go beyond that, like expressing emotions through the music, the experience of life events can help.

My life wasn't very straight forward. I had a long absence from my music. When I was living in the Middle East in my youth, and also after I left the Middle East, for a few years in London. I didn't know anybody in London. I threw myself into an unknown country as if I was a refugee.

But living in the Middle East, Japan and the UK and experiencing different cultures, listening to Japanese folk music, English classical music, rock music, pop music and also Arabic music helped my compositions. Without these experiences, I wouldn't have had the desire to write my own music. I just wanted to express my life experiences through writing music.

Do you feel there is still a harder path for women in Jazz music? Is this changing and do you see the future where gender will not be an issue?

TK: I don't think it's still a harder path for women in jazz music now. Many female jazz musicians are very active in the jazz scene, and they are doing very well. I don't think gender will be a big issue in jazz music in the future.

Can you see changes happening in jazz music—Are audiences growing, is there a thirst for more adventure in music do you feel?

Mainstream jazz is still very popular in UK, US, Japan and France. But nowadays, music media categorizes jazz as any music which has a tiny hint of jazz flavour, and also demands a young audience and young musicians who are looking for new jazz sounds. There is electronic, minimalistic energetic fusion running from the tradition of 'Sun Ra' to 'The Comet is Coming' with Shabaka Hutchings. This is music with a jazz flavour which is doing well and just one example of contemporary *Mercury Prize* nominee material.

If you could meet your younger self—just thinking of a career in jazz music, is there any piece of advice you might give her?

TK: If you think of a career in jazz music, it is incredibly hard to make is happen. I gave up the idea of a 'career' in jazz music a long time ago. If you are a young rising star in jazz music, you could be doing well for a while, but then you would be in a cloudy world; you would be lost.

There are lots of young musicians who went to a jazz academy and received a jazz degree, then went to teach in music schools. This gives better financial security.

I personally didn't go along the path of studying jazz in jazz academy and receiving a jazz degree. I am writing my own music and making CDs, finding gigs where I can play my own music. It's much harder to keep going. I have to believe in myself and I have to believe there are people who appreciate my music.

Given a blank canvas, just Taeko looking at the listening and interested world, what would you like to say to people who listen and come to gigs and buy your music?

TK: If people / listeners are prepared to put their preconceptions to one side and consider music that doesn't rigidly keep to a 'genre', then they can relax and interpret the output however they like. Jazz didn't move and change by being a 'rigid' genre.

♭ ♭ ♭

Melissa Aldana

"For me music is a purpose, a way to find the answer to the question, 'who am I?'. It is a way to find what I have to say, a way to release energy. I figured out that every time I play music, I want to feel completely empty you know, release energies and feel like I can completely express myself in a very free way and there is no judgment."

"It is hard to be living in New York. It was really hard to leave Chile; it was really hard to learn English. It is hard to wake up every day and try to practice to get better. I try to avoid some kinds of thoughts and try to be helpful, aware and encourage younger women but I don't let those things get to me to be honest."

Melissa Aldana is a saxophone player originally from Santiago, Chile. She performs with her band and as a solo artist. She is a graduate of *Berklee* and has played with luminaries of the jazz scene. Melissa's name appears on many lists of influential women in jazz. The daughter of a professional Chilean saxophone player, Marcos Aldana, she grew up immersed in the sounds of jazz and played in Santiago clubs in her early teens. She met Panamanian pianist Danilo Perez when he was on tour. He invited her to play at the Panama festival and she also attended auditions at several US music colleges. At *Berklee,* Melissa benefitted from the tutelage of musicians including Greg Osby, Jo Lovano, Ralph Peterson and Hal Crook. In 2013 she won the *Thelonious Monk International Jazz Competition* at the age of just twenty-three. With the award came a $25,000 scholarship and a recording contract with *Concord Jazz. The Washington Post* described Melissa as representing a 'new possibility and direction in jazz'. She was nominated a *Grammy* for best improvised solo.

In her interview Melissa discusses the influence of her father, her love for jazz, leaving Chile for the US, gender issues, living in NYC and much more.

The Melissa Aldana Interview

Who would you say influenced your early life, not just in music but you as a person?

MA: The main influence was my father. He was a saxophone player and my mentor since I was six. I learned from him the basics of the saxophone and so much more, like how to learn about language, what it means to have a good sound, what it means to have a strong sense of melody and harmony. Also, he taught me a lot about discipline. What does it take to achieve something in life? What does it take to follow your dreams? He taught me the importance of hard work; how it is important to live the process and try to master every little step of what you do in order to achieve something. So, it is not just about talent, it is about commitment. A lot of time is spent on your own trying to figure out what it is that you are looking for. He influenced me playing the saxophone, but he also influenced how I look at the process, not just music but also in whatever else I want to do. Discipline and commitment.

Your father was a professional musician and I understand it was your grandfather's Selmer MKV1 tenor you first played. What was it like having such musicians around when you were young? Do you think there was ever a choice as to whether you would play?

MA: My grandfather died when I was very young, but of course having my father around really influenced me playing the saxophone, but I remember I was strongly in love with the instrument from an early age. I was fascinated by the sound and especially around when I turned twelve and heard Sonny Rollins for the first time. That really opened my eyes and made me realize why I love this music with that kind of playing. With my father, I think I was extremely privileged to have this crazy man practicing six or eight hours a day, transcribing songs and repeating once, twice and maybe hundreds of times. Each melody, each transcription would be repeated until he played exactly how the person listened to played—which in those days was mainly Charlie Parker and Cannonball Adderley. This taught me so much about language and the importance of a sound and the feel from a very young age. I think I was mostly just very lucky to have had that kind of education.

Can you tell me what drew you to jazz in particular?

MA: Well, when I was young, I kept saying to myself, 'I play because I love it and it is just fun to do it'. As I grew older, I tried to find the meaning of what I do, not just in music but in life or for a purpose. For me music is a purpose, a way to find the answer to the question, 'who am I?' It is a way to find what I have to say; a way to release energy. I figured out that every time I play music, I want to feel completely empty, release energies and feel like I can completely express myself in a very freeway and there is no judgment. Also, for me, jazz is a way to communicate with musicians, maybe a little bit different than in other kinds of music. You are able to have a conversation, one on one in the moment and you are able to take so many decisions about the way you want to go. Nothing is right, nothing is wrong and that is one of the things I love about jazz the most.

Can you describe how playing the saxophone makes you feel what you think about the sound?

MA: You know the saxophone for me, not just the saxophone itself, but playing music, improvising, is a way to release energy, a way to empty. For example, when I have had a bad day and I am full of stress and I want to feel good. After playing a concert I just feel so much lighter and better and that is the best way I can describe it—a way to empty my emotions and just be free, just be in the moment. These days it is so hard to be in the moment and just 'be'. For me, though I try to meditate and other things, music is the truly the easiest way to be in the moment and just react to everything around. To react to whatever is happening around me. That is what playing the saxophone is to me.

Why did you leave Chile to study in the US?

I believed that if I wanted to be the best I could be, I needed to move to New York, which meant a move to the US. In Chile it is easy to become the best at what you do jazz-wise. People play at a high level and there are great musicians but I think there is something about living in New York, playing with those kinds of musicians, having that kind of experience, which really elevates your playing and allows you to go deeper into it. I know from an early age that if I wanted to be a jazz musician I had to live in New York for a good part of my life and get that kind of education; that kind of experience. When you live in New York you get your ass kicked. There are so many great musicians who play on a high level. It is so creative to be surrounded by these people and very important for me if I wanted to play at the very highest level.

What is the music scene like in the US?

MA: Well, more than in the US in general I look at New York where I live because there is so much variety. There are all levels and the best of the best lives here. I think that is the reason why we all live in New York—to get that kind of experience. I mean, to be able to just go outside every day and go to a great concert or play great sessions and be in a comfortable situation. That kind of thing is so important. The music scene in New York is very intense and very challenging but I think it is an important part of becoming a jazz musician.

I know you have played in clubs like Blue Note and also at festivals. How do you find the differences playing large or small events? Do you have a preference?

MA: Well of course, we all prefer small events in a small jazz club, as simple as possible, just because you can feel the people closer to you. You feel the energy differently, but one of the things I have worked on over the years is how can I feel the same on any kind of stage whether it's a big stadium or small or large venue. My approach to music is the same so the challenging thing is when it is a place where you do not feel as comfortable. You maybe cannot feel the musicians so close or the energy of the people. How can you bring the same kind of focus into the music? So, consistency is one thing I have been working on a lot and I feel like I have got it to the point where it doesn't matter what kind of stage it is, the feeling is the same. The approach is the same and of course you are always trying to do your best, which is the only thing you can play, I think.

Are there other events in your life which have affected your music? Do you think going through major events in life are useful and good for musicians or do you think they make you close down emotionally?

MA: No, I think they are good. I have been through a lot of heavy family things—issues with my father and mother—I mean, yeah mostly with my father. I don't want to get super-personal to be honest, but those events definitely changed the way I feel about myself and have brought me closer to understand who I am. I think that rather than be closed emotionally it is important to accept things and mostly what my latest album (Visions, 2019) talks about is the process of acceptance and embracing that through music. You know I don't have a relationship with my father, who was my mentor. I don't have my grandfather and it is about just being able to be okay with that rather than just kind of pushing my emotions away. I think it is an important part of growing up as a musician and that definitely comes into the music because you become confident with who you are. I think that those two things are very strongly connected.

Do you feel there is a harder path for women in jazz? Is this just in music? It is changing or do you see a future when gender will not be an issue?

MA: I can't ignore the fact there are gender issues. It is something that is there and there has been a whole history of inequality. I really haven't suffered with it, mostly because many older women have paved the way for my generation. I always believe that the most important thing is the music and that if you work hard and if your story is hard that comes across. That is the thing that I want to believe. That being said I probably ignored a lot of things in order to protect myself like I found out that maybe being female and being Chilean, meant I have been treated differently. That kind of plays against me and against the music. I don't want to be conscious of the, 'oh, I am different, maybe I play differently' thoughts. I just want to make it about the music and I think that the most important thing that I can do these days is to be a role model for younger women, which I never had on the saxophone. So yeah, I have never had an uncomfortable situation and never had to deal with those issues. Also, I think another part of it is that I have a strong personality and I don't let things get to me. The thing that makes me feel strong is if I feel good with my instrument and I am doing something meaningful.

It is hard to be living in New York. It was really hard to leave Chile; it was really hard to learn English. It is hard to wake up every day and try to practice to get better. I try to avoid some kinds of thoughts and try to be helpful, aware and encourage younger women but I don't let those things get to me to be honest.

What do you feel about education in jazz? Do degrees attract young people?

MA: Well, we all know these institutions are a big lie in a way. By that I mean you don't go to school and learn to play an instrument in four years. It doesn't work like that. You go to school to earn experience, to get a degree so you can hopefully teach, to get some lessons with great people, meet some younger musicians, or to get better. But I didn't learn how to play at *Berklee* and I didn't learn how to play in the US. I started at home with a lot of practice.

I assume you are talking about institutions and for me this system was helpful because it allowed me to travel from Chile to the US, get a full scholarship and be able to start my life here but I think the most important thing is what the person makes out of education. If you go to college and you are a musician you should have a clear idea about what you want to do. I don't mean like having a clear path but just being serious about your instrument— and that is what is going to make the difference to the kind of education you are going to get at the institutions.

Do degrees attract more young people? I think the reason degrees are good is that you can teach, so you have a back-up, especially as a self-employed person, this is an important thing.

If you are serious and your purpose in life is music of course you are going to keep playing. It is not something that is going to go away but maybe you find something related to music which may lead to a different place in life, a different career or just doing something different.

Can you see changes happening in the music? Are audiences growing and is there a thirst for more adventure in music do you feel?

MA: Well, those are hard questions to answer because all the artists are so different and there are audiences that are open to the music, others are not so open. There are some that are educated, others not so educated. It really depends. There is an audience in the US. There is an audience for specific kinds of music, whether *avante garde*, more traditional, modern or contemporary so I think there is an audience for everything. I am not sure if it is growing or not but from my experiences in New York there are a lot of young musicians and it feels like the music is really alive, at least around where I live.

Do you feel your Chilean background has an influence on your music style at all?

MA: Not really. I come from a country that doesn't really have a strong musical background like Argentina or Brazil. We do not have a strong sense of identity. Even though we have beautiful music going on and there have been a lot of beautiful and great artists it wasn't really part of my growth as a musician. I grew up thinking Charlie Parker was the hippest musician around because that is what my father taught me as a kid and I was never taught much about my heritage at high school, for some reason. So, I am not close-minded to the idea of exploring that but I don't want to do it just because I am Chilean. I want to do it because it is something that feels organic and there is a natural direction towards that.

How is your playing style received outside of the US?

MA: I feel very blessed and lucky that I am able to tour around the world and do what I want, play the music I want and stay true to what I believe I should be doing. That integrity is the most important thing for me. So, two or three times a year I play in Europe, I tour the US. I am constantly travelling and playing, mostly with my band and so far, it has just been great and I am very lucky to be in that place, especially during these times.

If you could meet your younger self just thinking about a career in jazz music is there any piece of advice you would give her?

MA: Not really. I have always tried to do my best since I moved to the US. I made a lot of mistakes. Of course, I can go back and think I wasted so much time but one thing I always did was practice. I always tried to get better and take care of the music and of course I still take care of the music—that is my life, my purpose. My purpose is not the career I have. That doesn't mean anything if I don't feel I am doing something meaningful. If I can't wake up and practice and feel like I am getting better and have something important to say the career really doesn't matter because I am not then being honest. Luckily, I can play the music I love and show my vision of how I want to be presented without sacrificing anything else.

What would you say to the people who come to hear you play and buy your music?

MA: Mostly I want to invite them on a journey. When I present a concert, I try to do it in an honest way, to represent our emotions, our mind's state, our influences. One of those for me is Frida Kahlo[24] who is the main inspiration for my latest album so I think that is the invitation, just to go on a journey with us and be open minded about interpretation in music. A lot of the music has stories behind which I often explain in concerts, like writers and books I have read and I like to share that to give an idea of how the music is composed. Thank you so much for having me as part of this, I really appreciate it.

Camille Thurman

"Every time I'm on stage, I am full of gratitude because it's an opportunity to be transparent and connect with people, using the gift to uplift people. The music is so healing, and you never know how music can heal or speak to someone in

24   Frida Kahlo was a Mexican painter who depicted life portraits and self-portraits influenced by the nature and culture of Mexico.

the audience."

"The only way gender is not going to be an issue is if we as a community put the work in and re-structure our understanding and use of gender roles in society, dismantling systems of patriarchy and replacing them with structures that support inclusion and equality."

"Sometimes you will have to put on your big girl pants and face uncomfortable situations, fears, and challenges."

"We as a community have to hold each other accountable for the intentional and unintentional gender biases we promote on a macro and micro level, including picking instruments. Children need to see both successful male and female musicians, bandleaders, composers, and educators. Young girls need to be in situations where they have fellowship with other female musicians and share their experiences, feelings, and insecurities, as well as moments of encouragement and empowerment."

Camille Thurman is a saxophonist who has made waves in the music industry. Her popularity is growing and she regularly tours, tops readers and musicians' polls and has won numerous awards. She is a member of the *Jazz at The Lincoln Centre Orchestra* and though she is known for playing tenor saxophone, she has been runner up in the *Sarah Vaughan International Vocal Competition*. She won the 17th *Independent Music Award for Jazz Album with Vocals* for her album 'Waiting for Sunrise'. She also won the 17th *Independent Music Award for a Jazz Song with Vocals* for her song 'The Nearness of You'.

Interestingly, although Camille was proficient at vocals, piano, and flute and attended *Fiorello H. LaGuardia High School of Music & Art and the Performing Arts* and learned the tenor saxophone form the age of 15 her bachelor's degree is in geological & environmental science which she gained from Binghamton University.

Here, Camille discusses her admiration for Dexter Gordon, collaborations, the communal nature of jazz and how traumatic experience led to her giving up playing for a period before taking up her saxophone again. Camille also discusses minorities, the lack of opportunities for them and the danger of discussions not happening if minorities are scattered throughout the industry and a lot more. Oh, and how to cope when a promoter thinks the correct way to present his business card is to stick it into your cleavage.

The Camille Thurman Interview

Who would you say influenced your early life—not just in music but you as a person?

CT: Dexter Gordon, Sarah Vaughan, and Ella Fitzgerald.

Dexter influenced me because of his confidence, wit and sophisticated approach as a musician. When I first started playing the saxophone, I was shy and not very confident about my instrument. I was the only girl playing the tenor saxophone in my summer jazz camp and it felt pretty awkward. Listening to him gave me the strength and confidence to try and not be afraid of playing.

Sarah and Ella inspired me personally and musically. Both were beautiful women that looked like me. I looked up to them because, when I saw their images, I saw talented women with beautiful chocolate skin like mine. They carried themselves with grace, dignity, respect, and confidence and were royalty to me. Sarah and Ella were my role models.

Can you tell me what drew you to jazz?

CT: Dexter Gordon and Sarah Vaughan drew me to jazz. Dexter had an incredible sound. He played in a way that was sophisticated but also humorous. He was also charming. He would play songs quoting various melodies, interweave them into his solo, and had a way of communicating with the band. I wanted to be able to have that confidence and add that richness of character to my playing. I knew from the first time listening to him play on 'Second Balcony Jump'[25] that I had to figure out that sound by any means necessary.

Sarah drew me in because she had a gift of using her voice as an instrument. She had an incredible range and, at the same time, was like Dexter in many ways. She was confident, witty, and sharp when she sang or improvised. I wanted to be that as a vocalist and instrumentalist.

Why is the saxophone your main instrument? Can you describe how playing this instrument makes you feel? What do you like about it?

---

25   'Second Balcony Jump' was a piece written by Billy Eckstein and Gerald Valentine and featured on Gordon's 'Go' album released on Blue Note in 1962.

CT: Originally, I started on the flute. I had brought a mouthpiece to my middle school band teacher, thinking it was a clarinet mouthpiece and he told me it was for saxophone. I immediately asked to play the saxophone, and he teasingly said, "No, finish learning the flute first" because two-three months prior, I had switched from trombone to flute. He proceeded to tell me that if I mastered the flute, saxophone, and clarinet, I could work on Broadway as a woodwind player. That immediately sparked my interest and I began to study the alto saxophone, along with the flute. I switched to tenor at the age of fourteen because I was offered a scholarship to a music preparatory school. The deal was if I could play tenor, I could attend the school for free. It just happened to be that my aunt's mother-in-law had a tenor in her closet, and she let me borrow it and eventually left it to me.

As a kid, I fell in love with transcribing Dexter Gordon's solos. It was as if I could lose myself in listening to him and transcribing him. I learned his solos by singing them and slowly but gradually began to transfer them to the saxophone. I wanted to figure out that sound, and the tenor had a rich and deep sound. I liked the alto sax, but there was something about the tenor that felt natural to play. I loved Dexter and I wanted my sound to be as rich as his, so the tenor was the best choice for me. The way Mr. Gordon played his horn gave me confidence and encouragement, especially during a time when I felt the most vulnerable, being a young woman—the only one many times—playing the tenor saxophone. My singing voice is naturally on the higher end, but the tenor enables me to tap into a different color and voice. There is a wide range of sounds to explore playing the tenor and singing. It's fun being able to communicate through sound with both instruments. It's the most liberating feeling in the world to be able to pick up an instrument and instantly speak. Sometimes words get in the way, but if you can hear something and instantly manifest it to sound, it's a feeling of freedom.

What is the music scene like in the U.S. and jazz in particular?

CT: Well, the music scene in the U.S. is diverse. We're in the age of the independent artist. Everyone has a product they're releasing with hopes to get it heard and distributed to the world. I think now the emphasis is on independent artists supporting themselves, using grassroots methods of building a fan base and getting the music out there through platforms that directly connect the consumer with the artist.

For jazz, it is the same. You have more people creating independent labels because the days of big record companies backing artists are gone. Recording artists have found a way to get to the demand directly through various platforms (social media, digital streaming, etc.). For many artists, including myself, being an independent artist takes a lot of responsibility, and you have to learn as much as you can about the business, to optimize your craft and make a living. This usually entails composing music, touring, recording and at the same time, operating as the manager, concert booker, producer, social media manager, web developer, and so many other things. It can be overwhelming, but with balance and good mentorship, it is possible. The most rewarding thing is learning how to manage myself and becoming a self-sufficient artist, that's empowering to me!

I know you play at festivals and club venues; how do you find the difference between playing in larger concert halls vs. clubs. Do you have a preference?

CT: I enjoy both large and small venues. The small venues are more intimate because you can directly connect with the people; make them a part of your personal space. Also, it's great for the acoustic setting because you can get to the real natural and organic sound of the band up close. I love large venues because the concerts feel like a giant party in your personal artistic and sacred space. The trick is to manage the balance of sound so that it is just as intimate but 'alive' in a larger setting.

The energy and love in both settings are beautiful to witness. Every time I'm on stage, I am full of gratitude because it's an opportunity to be transparent and connect with people, using the gift to uplift people. The music is so healing, and you never know how music can heal or speak to someone in the audience.

You have worked with some amazing musicians. How does this work when you are all playing at such a high level? Do you direct each other, work out your lines or improvise until the line is right? How does it work?

CT: Most of the time, if I am asked to collaborate on a project or a show, the musician organizing the project has a vision and maybe some musical ideas. We will try out some ideas. The whole process is trial and error. Most times, we don't know what to expect until it happens. Usually, when someone organizes a project with artists, they choose to work with the particular artists because they are familiar with the artists' artistry. When I organize projects, I always like to make space within the project for the artist to have room and be their natural and organic self. Sometimes things won't unfold the way we artistically envision them, and sometimes that's a good thing because the collaborative artist (especially an older one) might know just the right thing to do or know the right thing to add to the creative environment (that could be beyond my experience), which takes the project or artistic vision to the next level.

If it's a project that I am managing, my goal is creating an optimal artistic space where the main idea is present but the collaborative artists have room to express their self and be organic. Still, space is respectfully taken into consideration, allowing the artist to be who they are. Jazz is communal, not a dictatorship. Of course, talking through the concept with others is always a great thing to do and from there, we figure out as a collective who will do what and how will we start and finish. It's a loose, but structured process that allows for improvisation to be present, collectively and individually.

Are there other events in your life that have affected your music? Do you think to go through major events in life is useful and good for musicians, or do they make you close down emotionally?

CT: It depends on the person. I had to stop playing music after I graduated from high school. I went to a competitive performing arts high school and was discouraged, disappointed, and broken from a very traumatic experience. A few male musicians in our band made it very difficult for the few young girls that were there to play, and the administration didn't do anything to reprimand them because it wasn't a physical offense. This was before the *#MeToo* movement. It wasn't until I went to college that I picked up the saxophone again and was encouraged to sing and play. My college professor told me that I needed a safe place to learn that was judgment-free and nurturing. I grew so much while I was there and received the confidence, strength and healing that I needed to get back into music again. Going through this personal experience was necessary for my growth. It made me realize why I played and also made me vow to never allow anyone to mistreat me or push me in a place that denies me the space and opportunity to learn, be nurtured and creatively be myself.

Major events in life that affect musicians are sometimes used as a catalyst for creating art. I've known people who used life-changing events to be a catalyst for themselves creatively, musically, and personally.

Everyone deals with hardship differently. I've known people who went through major life events, and some of them chose to quit playing music. For others, they chose to work through it and keep playing. How an individual uses that experience to add or take away from their life is a personal choice.

Do you feel there is still a harder path for women in jazz music? Is this changing, and do you see a future where gender will not be an issue? Is the U.S. more difficult for women than elsewhere do you feel?

It is a path that is not without difficulty. First and foremost, you have to choose this path because it's your personal choice. There will be times that you feel alone, or you might not have someone whispering in your ear, "You're good, you got it, keep going." Sometimes you will have to put on your big girl pants and face uncomfortable situations, fears, and challenges. You have to love this music so much that you are willing to take a chance, whether it makes you money or not, whether it brings you fame or not. The most important thing is to be able to say, "I tried, I did it, and I learned something and I now know myself better than when I started."

I do believe that women face some disadvantages being female because of limitations or "standards" designed by society (image, body type, age, race, complexion, etc.), not just from men but from women as well. I'll never forget the time I was almost hired to perform in a band with a very well-known R&B singer, it eventually came down to the image 'concept' of what she was looking for in a musician and I didn't fit the bill even though I was qualified and had the experience. I was recommended by all of the horn players, and the musical director and I had the experience. Later, I heard stories of how some women in the same band were scrutinized because of their looks and weight. We, as a society, have to be conscious of how we uphold and practice standards of patriarchy that perpetuate gender bias, knowingly and unknowingly. We have to take an honest look into the system and actively set in place infrastructures that support inclusivity, not perpetuate exclusivity.

I believe the awareness of women represented in the arts is starting to initiate change and hold institutions and organizations accountable for including women. Conversations are happening on various platforms and allowing women to speak out and advocate for institutions to foster creative, safe environments that encourage inclusivity. The *#MeToo* movement has helped to get women to come together on a united platform and speak out against injustices. There is a voice for women now. For a long time, women didn't speak publicly about their experiences and encounters out of fear. Often women musicians did not speak with each other about the experiences we faced in the industry. We were spaced apart and didn't work together on the same musical platforms to have these conversations amongst ourselves.

On a community level, we still need the enforcement of women musicians represented at festivals, clinics, labels, master classes, lectures, grant selection panels and competitions. We also need to embrace women, without confining them to gender roles. As an instrumentalist and vocalist, people in this industry are not used to or familiar with dealing with an artist that does sings and plays. I think it's often taken as confusing to market me as a vocalist and instrumentalist. I had to figure out what to do with my other gift, singing. I kept it a secret for many years, out of fear. I wanted to prove myself as a strong player and not have people assume that I was only a singer. I had to work out who I was through my eyes, my identity, not through what was told to me by others. In high school some of the gentlemen were not kind to the ladies and I had to find a way of not allowing the situation to discourage me from believing that I could not play. I had to accept that I had a right to make mistakes, to learn, to take my time in learning and be the best that I could be. The pressure was hard to deal with many times, and it was a fight, but with the love and support of mentors and teachers I was able to go beyond and develop as a player.

Then there's the female part; men have done it, including Nat King Cole, Louis Armstrong, Louis Jordan, and Ray Charles, and a few women too, such as Vi Redd, Valaida Snow, Clora Bryant. The women who did both, unfortunately, did not receive the same attention, push, and notoriety as the men. There's a long history of women who were marketed only as a vocalist or pianist. Some of the well-known vocalists we know today were instrumentalists that were pushed into becoming vocalists because that was the most marketable thing to do. Today, you have women instrumentalists and you have vocalists, and then there's that small group of women who do both.

Sometimes it feels like a fight to do both, but I have no choice. It is my artistry and my path. I still feel that as a woman instrumentalist, it is a fight to be accepted, probably because, for so long, a platform was not given publicly for them but it is slowly changing.

I believe support is needed for the younger generation. It starts when students pick an instrument. We as a community have to hold each other accountable for the intentional and unintentional gender biases we promote on a macro and micro level, including picking instruments. Children need to see both successful male and female musicians, bandleaders, composers, and educators. Young girls need to be in situations where they have fellowship with other female musicians and share their experiences, feelings, and insecurities, as well as moments of encouragement and empowerment. I also believe that they should be surrounded by male and female role models and mentors. I had both as mentors and that encouraged and empowered me.

The only way gender is not going to be an issue is if we as a community put the work in and re-structure our understanding and use of gender roles in society, dismantling systems of patriarchy and replacing them with structures that support inclusion and equality.

I believe this problem not only exists in the U.S. It is a global problem. Often when I do tours sponsored by the State Department, I go on missions where the focus is outreach and women empowerment. In some countries, seeing a woman take on a leadership role (directing a band or playing front and center in an ensemble) is not often seen. It's a position of leadership that might not often be or at all displayed in some countries. We, as a global community, need to do better by creating opportunities for this to occur but also be seen regularly for both men and women.

So, are you noticing more women in the jazz industry?

In the last eight years, I've noticed more women instrumentalists in the jazz industry, but overall, there is still a need for them to be represented more on festival bills, performance venues, conferences, competitions, grants, panel discussions, and institutions. This does not happen magically; representation is what makes the difference. There were many women musicians that came before me, and I only know of them because I made an effort to find out and research them. Many of them did not get the same representation that many of us receive today, and these women paid their dues and helped the new generation of female instrumentalists to be where we are today. We still need more women managers, studio engineers, club owners, producers, promoters, and bookers in the industry. It takes the entire community as a whole to make this happen, as well as creating opportunities for women to fill in the gaps and be seen on a larger platform.

Do you have any particular stories where gender has played a part?

I have quite a few stories. I remember I was being honored for an award at an industry event. There was a man who was a promoter at the event and he was introduced to me by a male musician that I've known for a long time. Another male musician and his wife came to join the conversation. As we began to talk, the promoter asked about what I do professionally and proceeded to place his business card in my cleavage. The two male musicians looked away. I was in shock, embarrassed, and quickly pulled the card out of my cleavage and tried to shift the conversation. After the promoter left, the wife of one of the musicians said I did a great job handling the situation, but inside I was furious. I was furious because three witnesses were there and said nothing. I was complimented for 'being a woman' in the situation rather than being a person that was violated.

I also remembered one time performing at a party for a famous basketball player and was hired by a well-known saxophonist to play in his band. I'll never forget the look of shock on his face when I showed up with my horn ready to play. He ignored me and didn't talk to me during the gig. He allowed everyone to play solos, take away party gifts and gave them overtime pay and completely left me out. I even thanked him for the gig after the party, and he barely responded. I knew there was some friction, which I thought was ridiculous because we played the same instrument. Everything I was asked to do, I did well. I knew deep down inside that if I were a guy, it would have been a different outcome.

Can you see changes happening in jazz? Are audiences growing, is

there a thirst for more adventure in music do you feel?

CT: I see the audience growing. You have a younger generation of musicians taking advantage of social media and using it to connect with artists or, in some cases, put out information about the projects they are working on musically.

Globally, the audience is growing. I've been to Brazil, China, South Africa, India, and Australia this past year and have seen devoted fans that love the music. In some cases, they found a way to buy physical copies of albums that are not available for distribution in their country and many want the CDs autographed when a musician comes to the city.

I've had several people reach out to me via social media and express how happy they were to see me in performance settings either with my band or with the Jazz at Lincoln Center Orchestra. There is an excitement about seeing women in roles that aren't frequently seen in society or that have historically have not been represented. Music supporters and fans would like to see more women on the bandstand.

Do you feel education is important? How do you feel young people understand jazz and have a passion for it? Are women supported as well as other minorities?

CT: Education is extremely important. Young men and women need to see women in roles as bandleaders, instrumentalists, composers and arrangers to understand and see the possibilities that exist. Schools need to hire women artists to come and present their bands, host workshops, perform in school settings. Children need to learn about the history of women musicians as well as the male musicians that made accomplishments in jazz, including artists such as Mary Lou Williams, Valaida Snow, Lil Hardin Armstrong, and Melba Liston. If we can educate the community and value the accomplishments of men and women, it will inspire the next generation and teach the youth that this music is about the community.

Jazz contains a lot of rich social history that students need to learn and understand when navigating in today's world. This music was built on the experiences of black Americans living in America, the challenges they had to face, and how they made a living overcoming those challenges on a daily level. This music was one of the catalysts for integration during a time when it was illegal. Artists came together and spoke out against civil injustices and frequently used the music as a way to support the Civil Rights Movement. You have artists (Betty Carter, Charles Mingus) that were some of the first to ever independently own their labels and publishing companies, ushering in a generation of independent artists.

Unfortunately, I feel young people today learn jazz through a uni-dimensional way; the school. Jazz wasn't created in the school. This music was created by people who had to survive and face many challenges in the world. Their music is the story and reflection of how they overcame adversity and the lessons they learned living in this world. I believe teaching the history of the music along with the music itself will get students to see jazz isn't about competitions, licks or likes on social media. It will show them that this is creative community music that was used as a tool to bring people together and a door to expand possibilities and entrepreneurship.

Education and funding play a significant role, and this is one of the main reasons why it is a challenge to see young women continue to pursue careers in jazz. I don't believe women are as supported as they should be. Many times, they are not fairly represented in the industry. There are so many amazing women musicians on the scene that don't make the front cover of Downbeat or get featured on the big label or receive the press push for recognition, including the critics or readers polls. Often, the same group of women are featured and frequently lack diversity (i.e., race and instrumentalist vs. vocalists). For women instrumentalists, it is a fight to get coverage and exposure, particularly representation at festivals and clubs. It's also a fight to be signed and represented by booking agents, managers, and labels. Frequently, I look at the roster and don't see many women instrumentalists. Most of us are independently putting our projects out and are booking and managing ourselves.

When we speak about female minorities, that's another conversation. I feel it lacks the most when it comes to supporting increased representation of them. Whenever there is a women's movement, they are often overlooked or not included as much in the conversation. When we speak of representation, there are not too many women of color pursuing a career as jazz musicians because often, we face a lack of funding in our communities for arts programs that make it possible for young women of color to learn instruments. There is a lack of arts programs available in our neighborhoods, and there is also a struggle to obtain instruments and lessons that are affordable (for both young men and women of color). Most families are not financially able to support those essential things needed in the early development of playing an instrument. A woman of color is extremely fortunate to play an instrument at an early age, if she has access to one. Often, we start much later in our adolescent or teen years. Once young women of color start, they have to play catch up, especially if they're trying to get into competitive community school ensembles, a music college or school. This responsibility is completely on them. Young women of color are competing against students who have played longer, have financial support, family support, resources and have a track record of studying privately and playing in ensembles. To get an instrument in the hands of young women of color and for her to make it through high school, college, or as a professional is difficult. I believe it takes the community and educators working together to support, encourage, and create environments that are safe to learn and foster inclusivity (provide lessons, mentorship, opportunities to access instruments, see concerts) for young women of color to perform and study at an early age.

If you could meet your younger self, is there any piece of advice you might give her?

Put yourself first and invest all the time you can into your craft. If someone cannot respect your time and passion for your artistry, move on. Play with as many of your idols as you can. Learn from them and always have courage, even if you feel unsure or maybe scared of the outcome. Prepare, take a leap of faith, keep an open mind, play with people stronger than you and always keep moving forward.

I still believe it's a fight, and often "pure talent" is not enough. You can be amazingly talented, and I've seen push back because of societal standards influencing the decision of people to include or exclude women because of race, complexion, style, body type, image, sexual orientation, etc. As a woman in the entertainment industry, being good is not enough. You have to be smart and incredible at your craft. I believe there are glimmers of hope changing the perception of women and encouraging inclusivity. I am the first woman hired to perform and tour with the *Jazz at Lincoln Center*

Orchestra full-time for two seasons. Melissa Aldana is the first woman to win the *Thelonious Monk Competition*. Terri Lyne Carrington was the first woman to win a *Grammy* for the Instrumental Jazz Category, with Tia Fuller, who followed a few years later, becoming the second woman to be nominated for the same category. There are women out here picking up the mantle from where our "foremothers" left off and are running with it. This gives me hope and makes me push harder to make the change happen, hopefully inspiring the next generation to take flight.

Millicent Stephenson

"I know there are people who want to perform and want me to ask them but unless they can deliver there is no way I would put them on stage. It is my reputation at the end of the day. "

"I like the shape of the instrument, I like the levers, the springs, the felts. I actually went on a repair course so I can do some basic maintenance on it— that is how much I love it."

Millicent Stephenson is an in-demand, multi-award-winning full-time professional Saxophonist. Millicent is also an entrepreneur, songwriter, pianist, vocalist, music director, teacher, mentor, speaker and runs her label *Silver Gliss*. It might give more insight if I tell you about the period leading up to this interview. Before she gave her answers, Millicent gave me a message. "I want to apologies on how long it has taken me to do this. We had a conversation last week about how busy we are and I think sometimes I kind of don't notice that as much because my brain is always working, constantly whirling but it is like spinning plates, you know keeping them and sometimes some stop, hopefully not too many break, but life is busy as an independent artist. You've got to do your own PR, marketing, you know, keep your practice going, writing music, social media, thinking about where you are going in the future—there are so many things to think about (more apologies)." That tells you how busy Millicent is and also how she worries about giving her utmost to any project she is involved in. Millicent is an in-demand musician and founder of *Cafemnee*—a group which seeks the encouragement of female performers and Not Just Jazz—a regular concert series of shows.

The interview was well worth the wait and Millicent discussed her experiences in music, the amusing story of how she came to learn the saxophone, forming *Cafemnee*, hot flushes, motherhood, time management, the business of performing and so much more.

The Millicent Stephenson Interview

Who would you say influenced your early life, not just in music but you as a person?

MS: I had lots of influences in my early life. At school there were certain friends I hung around with who influenced me. I liked that they were confident, knew where they were going and what they were doing. I certainly lacked a lot of confidence in my younger days, but these friends were fearless. I had one particular friend who would always duck out of school at lunch time to go and buy a bag of chips for her lunch because she did not like the school dinners and I thought, "Wow! (laughs) That was so bold!" I remember trying it once, maybe twice, thinking as I walked down the street, "Oh, I am not supposed to be out here. What if I get caught? What if my Mum sees me?" So, I only did it a couple of times. It just didn't fit me at all.

Influences? I think one of the biggest influences was Andy Hamilton. I 'fell' into the saxophone and when I eventually met Andy Hamilton[26] I was very much at a crossroads with my music. I was in my early twenties and not a very confident woman, a sort of 'do as you are told type' of person, but really wanting to explore jazz and struggling to do that because the church I attended did not believe in musicians playing in pubs, clubs and places like that so that was a real tug of war for me. I remember having a conversation with Andy Hamilton and seeing him curling his lip—he had this way of curling his lip—well maybe not curling but he made this sort of 'N 'shape with his lips—like he wanted to say more but couldn't say a lot, but he really spoke to me a few times about really pushing out in jazz.

When ITV came to do a documentary on him called 'Silvershine'[27] I

---

26   Andy Raphael Thomas Hamilton, MBE was a Jamaican-born British jazz saxophonist and composer, who migrated to the UK in 1949. 'Silvershine' was a popular album and remains so today.
27   In 1988 EndBoards Production produced a documentary called 'Silver Shine' about Andy Hamilton's migration to the UK and the hurdles experienced in growing his music career, the changing musical taste of Windrush Generation and their descendants. The documentary features Andy's Band the Blue Notes with lead vocalist Ann Scott; his first youth band The Blue Pearls, Tony Sykes, Millicent Stephenson, and his children Graeme and Mark.

remember him inviting me to be part of it—to be featured—and I was so shy and so scared I said, 'Oooh, err... erm...' and on the day when they came I just didn't turn up. The following week when I turned up to rehearsal, Andy said to me, 'You didn't turn up!' and I said, 'I know, I just don't think I can do it'. He said, 'You have to do it and they are coming back'. So, they came back and I was there and they interviewed me and that was how I got featured on 'Silvershine' (laughs). So he is the one who really influenced me in terms of jazz. Then I decided not to pursue the jazz route because my faith was quite strong and I just didn't want to break any rules. It wasn't until much later as I matured in my faith and matured as a woman and got more confident that I realized that music is music and it depends on the context of the music—whether it is good or bad—and I then started to venture into jazz and when I played jazz I felt so free, so elated, like I was a bird flying in the air and it really kind of told me that jazz was something I needed to do, needed to play. I spent quite a few years learning jazz and morphed into playing other genres because I realized that as a musician you need to be versatile. So I play reggae, jazz, blues, gospel, little bit of rock. I have done classical stuff for when I did some exams so I think my style is very eclectic now. I include smooth jazz music in my set.

I have waffled and wondered off a bit there but we were talking about influences. Andy Hamilton was still playing when he was in his 80s and he didn't make his first recording until he was in his 70s, yet he was someone that kept music going even until the very end. He would invite me to go down to the *Bearwood Corks Club* where he was in residence and a couple of times I would turn up and he wasn't there… but his heart was there and he kept playing for as long as he could. So he was one of the main influences on my life.

Anna Brooks was one of my teachers. I met Anna when I was probably in my 30s. My children were a bit older and I decided to return to my music. I had taken a break from the sax when I had my son. When I had my daughter earlier it had slowed down a bit, so I wasn't gigging heavily and I was doing more keyboards and vocals, training choirs and things like that. I really liked Anna. She was a young woman with twins. Her boys were in primary school and she was pushing out in her music. She had very good parental support for child care, but it was good and very refreshing for me to see a woman who was making and owning music. I realized that I could do this too.

One of the biggest influences was my cousin Angela Christie. When I 'fell' into the sax around eighteen, nineteen years old, I went to Los Angeles with my cousin Carlton and he showed me her album and I listened to her play the saxophone. She was signed to a label and it made me think, "Wow!" because I had never seen a black woman play the saxophone. There was me and I had seen one or two of our friends, our age group who were just playing as a hobby really and we were eighteen, nineteen, but I had never seen a professional black woman playing the saxophone, so when I saw her doing it, I thought, "Actually, this is maybe something I could do".

I would say in my early days I was easily influenced. I didn't go off track and do anything stupid. I think I was a very quiet individual, certainly in my teenage and school years. I had my friends but I was lacking confidence. I am a middle child. I have three brothers older than myself, and three sisters younger than myself so I am in the middle. So, I feel a bit squeezed out from time to time with things and it is something I've had to overcome and work through.

Another person who influenced my life a great deal was a lady called Lorna George. I was in my mid-twenties and met her at work when I worked for the city council. We had loads of chats and conversations at lunchtimes and her being an older woman, probably five or six years older than myself, having a family, a husband, I really admired the way she thought and the way she handled management when they tried to pull a fast one, it was amazing. She gave me advice when I had conflicts at work and how to handle people.

Why the saxophone? I read that you first learned piano, then clarinet. Can you describe how the saxophone makes you feel, what you like about it, the sounds, anything?

MS: Well, the sax is just me. The saxophone is another limb to my body and if I don't play it for maybe 1, two or three days max I begin to feel as though something is missing and I get a bit cranky. It's a bit like a drug. The day I stop playing I don't know what will happen—I shall probably have to go cold turkey. I adore the instrument. I mentioned earlier that I 'fell into it'. What I meant by that is that yes, I learned piano; yes, I learned the clarinet; but the church I attended had a celebratory march and they wanted a brass band to lead the march and a friend of mine had trumpet and sax because he could play both. He was in a quandary as to which to play. I had a good friend, Lydia and we were chatting about this situation. I said 'Oh, I play the clarinet. It's the same family of instruments, I could do the sax'. The guy said 'OK' and gave me the sax. I took it—not very hygienic and not what I would recommend, but I used his mouthpiece and his reed to blow the instrument (big laugh). That's not a good thing to do, but I am still alive, so that's cool. So, I used his sax but when I took it home and played with the instrument and tried to figure out the notes and everything, I just felt, "Wow! This is definitely the instrument for me". I had played the piano, steel pans and clarinet and enjoy all of those but this one instrument resonates through my whole being. So that is how I came to play the sax.

What else do I like about the saxophone? I like the shape of the instrument, I like the levers, the springs, the felts. I actually went on a repair course so I can do some basic maintenance on it—that is how much I love it. So, I do a little tinkering on that side... I love the sound it makes, it's almost like singing. People say it is like the human voice. Sometimes when I finish playing my set and I go to sing—it really opens up my airways for singing and projecting. I really love it. It is very relaxing and it de-stresses me.

You have been involved in education. How do you feel about young people in jazz? Do you feel there is still the interest there was a few years ago or is this growing? Do you think education and jazz degrees make a difference?

MS: How do I feel about young people in jazz? The young people I teach— they don't actually say they want to learn jazz. That said, I have a nephew in his twenties and he loves jazz and wants to play it. In terms of students I teach, they tend to listen to a lot of pop tunes and mainstream stuff so they tend to be thinking about R&B and pop music. However, jazz is very much something you need to learn because by understanding jazz you can play almost any style. The good thing about jazz is the improvising and once you understand the rudiments of that, that is something that cuts across all the different genres and you can apply those techniques to your playing depending on if you are in a band or if you are soloing.

I don't teach at university level but I know there are jazz degrees and I know there are people who like jazz but if I had to guess I would say young people like to fuse it like the new-soul jazz type of vibe.

I don't think jazz is a dying thing either. I mean jazz has been around since the early '20s, '30s, '40s, and it is still going now. I think it is still alive and well. In the pop world you have the Ibiza style dance tracks and techno. The sax is used a lot in that and people do like the sax—that music is aimed at a younger audience so it is definitely there in clubs and places but regarding degrees I am not perhaps the best person to ask but I think it is down to tutors to educate the students. Another thing I would add to the subject of music degrees—whether it is pop, classical or jazz is that the business element is missing from the degrees and I think they are trying to build that in now. There are modules that talk about how to get gigs and how to get work, how to be a self-employed musician—these are things you figure out as you go along like I did, but degrees should help too. I have heard that some degrees now are putting in elements of this.

Tell me about *Cafemnee*—why did you feel this was important to set up? Has it been successful and is this ongoing?

MS: Yes, it's successful and yes, it's ongoing. Definitely. As a female musician I don't meet many female saxophonists. I don't meet many female keyboard players and very few drummers. They may play in orchestras, but in terms of the gigging world, there are very few that I have met, although there are female musicians around. It was a bit of an epiphany when I was at an event and down to play and was just listening to the music. It was a church setting and there was a female bass player, but I thought, 'Why is there no other female musician in this band?' Then I looked at the congregation and realized they were predominantly female. It got me thinking and I thought, 'Let me see if this is for real. Am I missing something or am I over-thinking it?' I contacted friends and other musicians—female and male—to see if this was their experience and they all said there were very few female musicians. There are statistics and reports to substantiate this, including national statistics from the *Musicians Union* and others, but it made me realize that here I am, doing my music, I need to get more females into music. Why are they going off the boil? I thought about the students I teach and I realized that I do teach quite a few girls, but when they get to secondary school what tends to happen is the individual music lessons have to be slotted into the timetable.

Parents tend to prefer their child to learn the core subject—maths, English—whatever they are doing, especially for GCSEs rather than doing music. My own daughter was in that camp. She was learning double bass and this was her experience with the timetable. I spoke to the school about the time of day when she could have a bass lesson and not be pulled out of the other lessons. It couldn't happen so I decided she would just have to do the additional work at other times because bass lessons were important. I found the teachers were pressuring her by saying things like 'well, if you miss this lesson, you may not be able to catch up' and other things. So, it was teachers who wanted her to give up music lessons. I am glad she didn't give them up. She is now playing well and enjoys her instrument.

Music is really important but there are hurdles like that in school. Then you get towards A-levels and degrees and it is another hurdle. Unless you are going to be a music student, doing music A-level or aiming for a music degree the other subjects tend to take priority. Women who go on to work in music, in orchestras or band, or as solo artists, if they start a family that means sometimes, they have to stop their music. Music may be bringing in income so they lose that and they have to juggle unsocial hours, child care and so on. In my mind, I knew there needed to be more women in music. So, I set up *Cafemnee*. We had our first meeting and around nine people came. We have been growing ever since. We are in our fifth year and twice a year, I hold workshops and we have the website and I share opportunities I come across with the women. It has been successful. I did an article for *The Voice* newspaper and that was picked up by the *BBC 1* for their *Songs of Praise* and they used myself and *Cafemnee* for the *Zeebrugge* episode in 2017.

One of the things I really like about *Cafemnee* is the growth in the women. When the women first started, when we had a jam session it was like a real struggle. Women were not certain about how to do a jam, how to improvise. They didn't really understand how to develop and create a music career. Over the years we have covered a variety of topics. 'Play it like a man?' was one topic; and one was 'how you dress and your appearance'; 'your mind is your music' where I brought in a psychotherapist to talk about some of the mental things we go through to get on stage and how we can improve... We have covered social media and we had an open mic feedback session recently. That was pretty good and the women had the opportunity to perform a song of under three minutes and get feedback from a supportive panel and it was great. It was so fantastic seeing the women going up there confidently, setting up their stage, performing their song, taking the critique and a few minutes later, they had the opportunity to go back up and apply one thing they were told about. They applied it and it worked. It was fantastic. Outside of the organization we have women now who confidently go to jam sessions, joining bands, performing, one lady is running an agency, they are getting paid work so yes, *Cafemnee* is successful, it is going and it will keep going as long as I can keep it going.

How does being a wife and mother fit in with your musical career? Have there been times when it has been difficult to adjust to the role.

MS: I have two children. They are both adults, my son is twenty-five, my daughter twenty. When I was pregnant with my son, I was able to play the saxophone up until about five months and then there was no space for baby and blowing sax. So, I stopped playing. Then he was born and I practiced once a week, played when I could, but I didn't do a lot of gigs. I did other forms of music. When my daughter came along it was a similar thing. The sax took a back seat for a while. In fact, when I was engaged (I have been married twenty-nine years) I was performing each week and my husband was in Manchester, so I moved to Manchester and had to come back to Birmingham for gigs. It was not like now where you can set up gigs using the Internet—it was all phone, but it got to the point where my husband was fed up with travelling and I wanted his company but didn't want to be travelling on the motorway on my own and so on. I had to turn down gigs and in Manchester at the time there were few outlets for me to play in. But when my children got older and went to secondary school, I began to feel like there was a lift and I could get my life back—not that I didn't love my children and being a Mum, but as Mum, you are it in terms of childcare and support.

I began to think about getting older and it would be a huge regret of mine to have not had one last push on the saxophone to see if I could do it. I spoke to my husband about it to see if I could give it a go. To be fair ever since the day I started playing jazz and since Andy Hamilton's encouragement (even though I perhaps chose a different direction and even later than that), there was always this internal push inside me to play jazz, to do music. I think I was created to make music (pauses to take off tracksuit top and jokes about menopausal flushes amidst laughter).

So, I felt I needed to give it a go. My husband agreed with me which was great. I think if he had not, I might still have given it a go, but I am glad he supported me. I was doing a lot at the church and they released me and agreed I should give it a push. Age was a consideration—what does a thirty-nine year-old woman do in music? So, I gave it five years to see what I could do. Five years have come and gone. I am now fifty-six and opportunities still keep opening up. Age is just a number. If you have what it takes, if you present yourself well and keep developing your playing so it gets to a high standard, your standard, and you've got a bit of a business mind set, you can make it. I don't believe age can hold you back. It certainly didn't hold me back. There are people who achieve things in later years and I guess this was my time.

Fitting things in was hard. In the early days I had to wait until Michael came home or could take the children out before I could go to the studio or practice. I couldn't practice when the children were there—that just does not work. My husband is understanding and very supportive. He comes to gigs; he does the driving; he sets up the PA system so I can get changed. If I have hurdles in the business, he gives his opinion as he is in business himself. My children often come with me and they are great at taking pictures and handling the social media. They have loved seeing their mum develop as a musician.

Have you ever heard someone play and been totally blown away by what you are hearing?

MS: Maceo Parker. I love the way he vibes. I have listened to the way he plays and his songs. I listened to one where he played more or less three notes but the improvisation around them was amazing. The way he builds it up and the way he changes keys, just amazing—I have to find that track again. I listen to Andy Hamilton, my tutor. I loved the way he played. I remember hearing a sax player on Radio 4—she was a female sax player. She was playing in WW2 and I listened to her play and thought "wow- great tone". Other players like David Sanborn, Cannonball Adderley—quite a few sax players. I just like parts of what they do in songs which is mind blowing but sometimes, not a whole song. I love Tina Turner. She does a song called 'Complicated

Disaster'—just Tina doing her thing. I put it on in the car at full volume. I love the structure, the chords. In terms of sax playing, there are aspects of what certain people do which I love.

You run your own label—how does this fit with your creative side? How did you learn your business skills?

MS: I learned business skills when I left secondary school. I did a BTEC National in business and finance. I went on to do a BTEC HNC and then my degree was in computing with an element of business. I also ran a business with my husband—we had a training company, which we ran together though it closed in the recession. Also, when I was at school, I learned commerce. I was fascinated by the whole concept of the stock exchange and business so I have always had an interest and because I had that background and experience of running a training company it made me confident in running the business side of my music. That is the thing which has made my music successful. I make sure I apply the business approach to everything I am doing. That is a message I would give to anyone. The label side? To be fair that is just admin. It is not creative really. For example, once you have written a song and recorded it, you then have to register it on different platforms and that is the admin side. It is a bit like pulling teeth really and not that enjoyable but it is important if you want to get your music out there and for people to find it and make sales. I am still learning skills, still learning now and I pick things up as I go along. I also go to some training courses which *Musicians Union* put on or *Federation of Entertainment Union* (FEU), internet training too. Business skills are very important, but I like learning.

When you founded Not Just Jazz[28] were you surprised it sold out before the opening gig?

MS: I was surprised—definitely.

Does this perhaps suggest that there is an untapped thirst for good

---

28   'Not Just Jazz' showcases Millicent's original compositions as well as her interpretation of iconic Jazz, Blues, Reggae, Soul and Gospel numbers with her live Band, backing singers and dancers. Her fans described the night as 'captivating', 'uplifting' and 'entertaining'. Millicent featured the National Caribbean Monument Charity in Not Just Jazz III and Not Just Jazz IV. The charity is campaigning for the erection of a memorial in the Staffordshire National Memorial Arboretum in remembrance of Caribbean Military heroes.

music by people? You hear of venues opening and closing on a regular basis but do you think people are missing chances to create spaces which could be commercially viable if they chose the right acts (as NJJ surely proved).

MS: I think so. It was my first one and I think what surprised me was I have a fan base—and this is about learning business. I did not understand the concept of a fan base until four or five years ago. I just played and played and people were saying 'Where can I find you? You are really good and I want to hear you again' and I didn't really have any where they could find me on a regular basis. I tried a few restaurants to see if I could get a residency but it was at the time when the recession was doing its thing so that didn't really workout. I just thought, 'you know what? Put on your own show. Just do something and see what happens.' So, I put a show on in the bar of the *Crescent Theatre* and it sold out. Then I realized how much people like what I do and that I can do it very well. I could put on my own show. So, the show has now been going for six years. In its fifth year, we had a photographic exhibition and did not do the concerts because one of the ladies who works with me lost her mother and at the same time my husband's father became extremely ill. It was too much for me to do it all, so we had the photographic exhibition where the photographer (Anthony MacFarlane) put on works of me. The year just gone we did the show and I realized people want to see me and want more so this was a lesson.

Regarding creative spaces—I think it is about getting good acts into the venues. It is about the prices that are charged for drinks or meals. It is also about the rent or the lease, fees and everything else. The business has to balance. Sometimes venues reduce the rates they pay to the musicians to make the most amount of money, but if the musicians perform well, then people are going to buy drinks, they are going to buy food. So, there is a decline of music spaces and people go out less. Also, people can watch on the internet. But live music is live music. You cannot exchange the vibe, the atmosphere, the emotion, the connectivity and the feel-good factor you get from listening to a very good band and watching the performance. It lifts the mind and relaxes people and sometimes, they want more and more.

How do you choose acts to put on at events? What do you seek in players?

MS: first of all, when I first chose acts, it was people I knew who sang or played really well. The last show I did I had some of my *Cafemnee* women as the opening acts and some formed a band and opened the show. It was really good. I coached them on stage performance and it was great. They still play and are really good. I think going forward I may choose larger acts with a following. Again, it is business and you want to increase footfall and whilst you want it to be a good night, you have costs and it should not come from your pocket. I do not choose acts that cannot deliver. Never. I know there are people who want to perform and want me to ask them but unless they can deliver there is no way I would put them on stage. It is my reputation at the end of the day. I should also add that I know some very good singers and performers who I have not asked because you can only ask one at a time really. But I have a list and going forward I shall be asking.

Are there other events in your personal life which have affected your music? Do you think going through major events in life are useful/ good for musicians or do they make you close down emotionally?

MS: So, I will say here about menopause and gynae problems. I don't think I have read many articles about pregnancy etc. and the effects on female musicians' work. I think, as women, we have something that happens to our body once a month. Usually, it does not get in the way of anything we do because as a teenager maybe you learn to look after yourself, but it is a fact. Your body changes and your emotions change according to your hormones. As a musician you have to try to put that aside and perform even if you feel terrible. About seven years ago, I had fibroids and that had an impact on my music because I had to be checking my dates, prepare myself and be comfortable. It is a common thing, especially with Afro-Caribbean women. It was difficult but I was careful about taking gigs at certain times. I had an operation and my tummy was swollen so it may have looked like I was pregnant. I had to choose my clothes carefully to disguise the swelling. I had an operation and then felt awful. I lost confidence and took a few months off. I kept things quiet. My recovery was slow, I felt low and had pain; but as I began to feel better and heal, I began to feel better about myself, even *good*. I felt my confidence rise. Then I had the menopause. So, sometimes I take a small cloth in case I have a hot flush. I have a little hand held fan on my music stand but I don't care now. It makes me comfortable. I remember talking to my friend Pat and she said to me 'You know, when you see recording of performers like Mahalia Jackson or Tina Turner and they are sweating profusely, who knows, maybe they were having a hot flush rather than their body creating a lot of heat with the work.

For me, menopause has not greatly impacted my life. I do not have to rush out of bed in the mornings often. So if I have had a sleepless night because of the impact of symptoms, I have the choice to rest. Most of my lessons are later in the day. I have made a few adjustments, like having a spare outfit and watching what I eat just to restrict any sweating or other symptoms. So personally, that is something which has affected me, but I am not embarrassed by it. I have friends who get embarrassed, but I just think, 'Why? This is normal.'

Do you feel it is still a harder path for women in jazz music? Is this changing and do you see a future where gender will not be an issue?

MS: Well, I would love there to be a future where gender is not an issue. I think women have it harder whether you are in jazz, rock, folk or whatever. Let's take appearance. In the pop world it is presumed a woman will reveal more of her body than a male counterpart. If you look at the top 20 female pop artists, they probably wear next to nothing whereas a man can just put on a shirt, a pair of trousers, glasses, a nice sheen on their bald head or put a cap on and they are good to go. Women have to think about the false eyelashes, make-up, jewelry, do they wear a wig or not, what do you tuck, what do you lift, what size heels? We have all these things put on us and it is unfair. In the jazz world there is not so much pressure as you are judged more on your ability. But there are reports, certainly the *MU* have these reports from women who have been harassed. I remember listening to one woman who was in a recording booth and a man who she liked just came in and kissed her. She was taken aback because she was working, but some men feel they can just cross boundaries just because you are a woman and look good. That is quite unfair. I have had a couple of incidents where at the end of performing some people want to take pictures. I stood by a particular dignitary whose hand slipped from around my waist to my rear. I was shocked because he was a man of some standing. I think most women have tales to tell and I am looking forward to the day when gender is not an issue. It was one of the reasons, I set up *Cafemnee* because I think the more we have women in the industry, the more the balance will change. The more women we have in higher positions, the more it will change. It is also one of the reasons I am on the *Midlands Regional Committee* of the *Musicians Union*, why I went on to the equality sub-committee of the union. Just last week I was appointed to the executive committee of the *MU* so I am now part of the committee which makes decisions for the *MU*. I want to see equality and fairness for women in music.

There are reports of festival line ups with no women or just one woman on the bill and when you look at the top twenty in the pop charts, sometimes it is just 1 or two women who are there. There are not a lot of women in the industry as a whole.

Do you notice differences in the music scenes (jazz) in the UK and elsewhere, even in the UK itself? Where do you see the UK music scene of the future?

MS: I can't see a noticeable difference. I would love to see a thriving, healthy music scene in the UK. It would be great to see fair pay for musicians who are playing across the UK, whether in a pub of Wembley Stadium. I would like to see this because many times musicians are not paid what they are worth and end up doing another job as well as playing. It is about affording to be able to play. I would like to see good degree courses and also music at A-level where music is seen as a viable career option and where people can choose not to just be performing artists, but maybe work as part of organization like in the *MU* and record labels. I would like to see the benefits of music promoted—how it helps children in their learning and individuals, how important it is to have music at events and why we should pay musician properly. I would like to see a strong, competitive music scene.

If you could meet your younger self—just thinking of a career in jazz music is there any piece of advice you might give her?

MS: I would tell her it's going to be all right; it is going to work out. Delaying going into jazz was not a bad idea because at that point I was not confident. At the same time, who knows? Had I chosen jazz at a younger age; would my music career have been further down the road earlier? However, it is what it is. I might tell her to speak to different people in the industry—be confident, trust yourself. Jazz is a really good art form to learn and understand. Maybe find a good teacher even earlier to learn about music, extended chords, improvisation.

Given a blank canvas, just Millicent looking out at the world, what would you like to say to people who listen, come to gigs and buy your music?

I usually say things to them when they come but I think I would say treat everyone fairly, think about how people feel, try to make wise choices with your life. Have fun at gigs. To be kind, especially drivers. I would like to see fewer road hogs and for people to care more. Support live music venues and buy music to support artists.

Jane Bunnett

"Sometimes people call music 'jazz' and I can't for the life of me hear any improvising going on which is supposed to be one of the most important things in jazz."

"If you really want to be a jazz artist, out there performing, you have got to be up for the adventure. You must search out your musical heroes."

Jane Bunnett is a saxophonist and flautist. She is holder *of Canadian Medal of Honour* and plays across the world. Her *Maqueque* project brings Cuban female musicians to the fore and has proved incredibly successful. In 2004, Jane was appointed an *Officer of the Order of Canada*, the highest civilian honour given to Canadian citizens. Recipients are those who show 'outstanding achievement and service to the country or to humanity at large.' In 2006, she was awarded an honorary doctorate by *Queen's University* at Kingston, Ontario, Canada. Her husband is trumpet player Larry Cramer, who also acts as manager and takes on various roles for their frequent visits to Cuba. Her awards for her music are many but include several *Juno Awards, Grammy* nominations, *Downbeat Critics' Awards, Jazz Journalists' Awards*, a *Smithsonian Institute Award* for contributions and dedication to the development of Latin Jazz and many more. In her interview Jane discusses many things including getting more recognition for female musicians in Cuba, visas, working relations with husband Larry Cramer, social activism and the role of women in jazz.

The Jane Bunnett Interview

You have worked with musicians including Don Pullen, Sheila Jordan and Paul Bley. For each musician you work with, is there a period of adjustment to their character, how they understand and interpret your way of playing or is it simply a matter of picking up your instrument(s) and playing?

JB: These musicians were heroes of mine and my husband Larry. At the time of working with them it was a period when I was seriously focusing on their music. I was trying to find my own voice in collaboration alongside what they did. I submerged myself deeply into their music, listening to many of their recordings so I was thoroughly informed. Paul Bley did not want me to over prepare but hah! That was easy for him to say. He had played with everybody.

Dewey Redman, who we worked with a lot, was very open to ideas and that was really great. He, like many artists we were playing with at that time, embraced the traditional but could play *way* outside that too. Dewey had played with Ornette Coleman and many others. He was a wonderful artist we worked and toured with. When I prepared for my first recording in my late '20s called 'In Dew Time' (Dark Light, 1988) I spent years preparing and listening to the artists that would be on the recording—Don Pullen, Dewey Redman, French horn player Vincent Chauncey and Canadian drummer Claude Ranger[29]. I was jumping into the fire—but that's how you grow as a musician. All of these artists demanded only that you play with honesty and tried to sound like you. That is a great lesson even now. When I work with musicians outside the Cuban scene there is always a bit of a shift and preparation to take on a new project successfully.

---

29   Claude Ranger was a drummer with a reputation for incredible playing but who mysteriously disappeared aged 59 in 2000.

*You have worked for 30 years or more with Cuban women and music.
Can you describe to me how this started? What was the situation in
Cuba and how did you find the women for the Maqueque project? What
was the inspiration and aspiration?*

JB: My first trip to Cuba was in 1982. That was mind-blowing. We went to
Santiago de Cuba which is on the eastern (Caribbean) side. There, they have
very different sounds than those of Havana and the area is the home of Cuban
'son'[30], '*changuí*'[31] and the *comparsa*[32]. These are the musics of the carnival. In
four hours, I heard five different genres of Cuban music. I had no idea that
this musical journey would turn into life-long musical collaborations and
discoveries. Three weeks later we visited Havana. We met a 'who's who' of
the music scene there. It was like discovering a gold mine. There were endless
possibilities and musicians who were game and up for collaborations. We
began—after many, many trips over the next few years—to plan our first
Cuban recording. At this point we only had our debut LP 'In Dew Time' out.
We prepared like crazy.

After meeting the great vocal artist Merceditas Valdes[33] (a highly influential
Afro-Cuban vocalist) and her drummer husband Guillermao Barreto (a major
figure in Cuban music) we made field recordings on my little Sony cassette
player, of folkloric groups, specifically *Grupo Yoruba Andabo*. I brought them
back and worked on bringing harmonic elements and arrangements into the
mix. This was such an exciting time. I took the arrangements back to Havana
to present them and play along with the musicians. It was thrilling. This first
record, 'Spirits of Havana' (Linus, 1993) was a ground breaking recording
that opened many doors for me internationally as nobody had really done
anything like this. At the time, it was such a hard project to do as we were
foreigners, prohibited from going into the *Egrem* studios (Egrem has been the
national label of Cuba since 1964, with headquarters in Havana) and *Grupo
Yoruba Andabo* were registered as dock workers, not professional musicians.

---

30   Son Cubano is a music which features characteristics form Spanish and African music. Using
vocals, dance and a lyrical metre from Hispanic origin and clave rhythms and call and response structure
which originate in Bantu culture. It became popular in the highlands of eastern Cuba in the late 19th
century.

31   Changüí is music which arose in the sugar plantations of Cuba, especially in Guantánamo
Province and was characteristic or rural slave communities where many inhabitants worked in the sugar
plantations. It is a fusion of African and Spanish music.

32   Comparsa applies to groups of dancers and singers in carnivals.

33   Merceditas Valdes (1922-1996) was a highly influential Afro-Cuban vocalist

Only state sanctioned musicians were allowed in the *Egrem* studios. We had Gonzalo Rubalcaba (an Afro-Cuban jazz pianist and composer), Hilario Durana (a Cuban-Canadian jazz pianist) and the great Frank Emelio (an afro-Cuban jazz pioneer, most known for his small ensemble work) on our first Cuban CD. Wow! That was a coup.[34]

Merceditas Valdes and I were the only women beside all these amazing musicians and that's how it remained for many years. After the passing of Merceditas in 1996 and in our 'Sprits of Havana' group (which was established in 1990), I have always been the only woman in the groups.

It has been 29 years now and the group has been a platform for many young, talented male musicians from Cuba that have passed through and gone on to establish their own illustrious careers. To name just a few these include David Virelles (jazz composer and pianist), Elio Villa Franca (jazz composer and pianist) Dafnis Prieto (drummer, composer, bandleader and educator), Francisco Mela (drummer and percussionist), Pedrito Martinez (percussionist, drummer, singer, dancer and band leader) and Yosvany Terry (saxophonist, percussionist and composer). No women until now. Also, during this time, we established an organization called Spirits of Music. This came about because of visiting the music schools in Cuba.

There are twenty-five well-organized conservatories and I kept meeting many young women in their programs—they get a good fifteen years of training, starting at eight years old. They graduate pretty much as professional musicians, yet I never saw any of these young women out on the scene playing afterwards. They seemed to be content (or not) to observe from the sidelines—and watch their boyfriends have all the fun. Even though I tried to encourage them to get up and play alongside me, I could not make that happen. In 2014, I felt it was time to see if I could assemble a group to record a project. With the help of a young vocalist called Dayme Arocena, I put *Maqueque* together for what I thought would be just a one-off project. *Maqueque* means 'fiery energy and spirit of a little girl' in Afro-Cuban dialect. I quietly went down to Havana and looked and listened to the different female players. I chose them for their enthusiasm for improvising, their musical force and personalities as this is important.

---

34   In 2000 the story of *Spirits of Havana* was made into a *National Film Board of Canada* film by directors Luis O. Garcia and Bay Weyman.

The first recording was a difficult one because all the players were at different levels, some with hardly any improvising chops, but they had the spirit. This recording moved from different studios as things broke down—a common occurrence in Cuba. Our rehearsal sessions took place in a club where the electricity kept going off. We would just sit in the dark—less than ideal. Anyhow, the record ended up receiving a *Juno* award in 2015 for best contemporary jazz so maybe we were on to something. The rest is history as the group is now being touted by *Downbeat Magazine* as one of the best 10 groups touring at the moment.

You work with your husband, trumpeter Larry Cramer. How does that work? Is Larry involved with your projects? I know he is the main contact when people reach out to you. How did you start to work together?

JB: Well...one of the things is we have the same email...ha..ha!

We joke about things because he produces our recordings and is the producer of *Maqueque*. So, he produced himself out of the band. He was in the original band on 'Spirits of Havana' but he was also always behind organizing the logistics of getting from A to B and the financial framework of how we should tour, the production costs etc. He has pretty much been the mastermind from our very first disc.

Larry organizes so much—where we bring the musicians together from different locations, where we rehearse, where everyone will stay, and the flights. He organizes live shows and when we go into the studio he organizes and deals with costs there. It's a lot of work. But we work as a team and he gives me my chores too, which I happily agree to do because, as I said, we are a team. To be fair though he deals with *way* more than me.

From the very beginning, even when we started to date forty-two years ago (yikes!!). He was the planner, dreaming of how we could make things happen for us as a couple in music. Many times, he has taken a back seat and watched from the sidelines and cheered me on. But everyone who knows us well understands that I could not have accomplished things this far without him. I am an extremely lucky person.

On Wikipedia you are described as a 'social activist'. To you, what does this mean?

JB: I was brought up to care about people less fortunate than myself. I would say I grew up in a pretty nice family environment. My parents made us aware that many others did not have the same upbringing. So, from an early age and witnessing especially my mother's involvement in many issues as a child, I was aware of helping when I could.

I feel as a musician my assistance can be used in many ways to reach people— to grab their attention for social injustices, or even just raising money for organizations that represent a possible improvement in people's lives. It's what I do best and of course it is a powerful tool to get people's attention. There are many causes that I care deeply about and I never hesitate to jump in and lend a hand if I can. I might not have the money to give, but I can always use my talent and bring other musicians on board so that we collectively can assist with generating the necessary money. People know me for this, but I do choose carefully which organizations I work with.

In 2020 you have the Safari Project in Cuba. What is the project about and what does it aim to achieve? Are the women you work with in Cuba free to travel?

JB: We are guest curators of this 'Jazz Safari to Cuba' on behalf of our 24-hour not-for-profit jazz radio station here in Toronto, *Jazz 91 FM.* Every year we take a large group of people who have donated operating money to the station to Cuba. In return for their kindness, the donors receive a tax receipt for their donation and get a one-week trip to Cuba where we expose them to the beautiful Cuban culture, music and art. It's a terrific trip and a win-win situation for all.

Your question about are the women free to travel is tricky. We travel all over the world with them. We have recently done two tours of Europe, and just came back from the Dominican Republic, Argentina, and we tour the USA (but this is extremely challenging under the embargo). For everywhere we go, we must apply for visas so there is a lot of waiting time and costs. It is very tricky and exhausting, but we do it because we have to get our music out there.

Have you found music changing at different levels and in different ways in different places? Cuba, Canada, US, Internationally, how does jazz sit in the world?

JB: I think the music has changed in some ways. There is the old good music versus bad music. There are a lot of other influences now in jazz like world sounds, the spoken word or rap, electronica, *et cetera* everywhere. You might find a certain sound has a bit more of a popular outreach if it's smooth jazz or dance music. Sometimes people call music 'jazz' and I can't for the life of me hear any improvising going on which is supposed to be one of the most import things in jazz.

Well—and this is a hard thing because I just know what I like—I am still a purist, but I like to hear new things as long as the music is honest, has heart and soul, is original and creative. I think that's why our group *Maqueque* is reaching people. It is because of all these reasons. We are not straight ahead jazz, but we are rooted in Cuban musical rhythms—with a lot of improvising, and we are original. No-one sounds like us.

Do you feel women have a part to play in changes in jazz music and the industry?

JB: I sure do. Women have always been in jazz music; they just have not been recognized enough. We of course need to always welcome more women into the fold. This starts with having more women involved not just as musical artists, but on every level of music—production, artistic direction etc. Then it will be a lot more balanced.

If you were to meet your younger self, just contemplating a career in jazz, is there any advice you might pass on?

JB: There are many more possibilities in the jazz world now. There are directions that you might go in that were not around when I was starting out. If you really want to be a jazz artist, out there performing, you have got to be up for the adventure. You must search out your musical heroes. I feel I followed my head and heart and I never took 'no' for an answer. I guess I might have wished I had borne down sooner and worked a little harder in my late teens, but I was a creative person and I wanted to search around out there. I guess, in truth, that time made me the person I am today. I hope this shows through in my approach, sound and output.

♮ ♮ ♮

Arema Arega

"If you stretch your hair, you will look like a white person."

"I like jazz because it's not one thing. Jazz has many genres within itself. It represents freedom and I love it when I can walk at the edges."

"So, my main advice would be to be persistent, focused, to be true to yourself. Defend your ideas, while at the same time, be aware of the signs and advice that life offers. Learn from every experience, because our journey is a lesson. Share your light with good people, and wish and do well by others in every instance, because there is always a way for those who pursue a dream."

Arema Arega is a Cuban singer, fashion designer and musician living in Madrid. Arema is fast becoming a much sought-after musicians—from pop to jazz to native instruments she is fluent on many instruments and in many genres. She is also an artist and involved in film projects. I have spoken to her when she has been out of breath, trying to get to the school on time to collect her son but still working at her music and she is the kind of person who sends you a virtual hug and tells you to keep going like she does, even on those days when it can feel like a lot of hard work and little feed-back. She celebrates other people's success and believes in a positive energy and light we can all tap into. In her interview, Arema tells of the time she sang for Sting, her convoluted travel arrangement to return to Cuba form Spain to find her son, her time as a seller of bakery products on the street and some very fortuitous meetings with people who spotted her talent and encouraged her.

The Arema Arega Interview

Who were your influences when you were young—not just in music but in your life.

AA: I was born in Russia and went to Cuba with my mother when I was three months old. My mother was deported for having a relationship with a foreigner. That was my beginning in this world of travelling. My first influence was my family—my mother, grandparents and uncle. Also, I was somehow influenced by those who were absent—in this case my father and his family. I only met one of my father's sisters when she came to study medicine in Cuba.

I was about five and then she left. We got in contact again when I was twenty-seven and my first child was three.

I think the stories we grow up with are part of our life-lessons and my mother always made me proud of being half Cuban and half Ethiopian, telling me what she knew about my father, his family, his culture and about the beauty of being black. It may seem strange because Cuba is a multiracial country but there is a lot of racism. My mother's teachings helped me to feel good about myself living surrounded by comments like, "if you stretch your hair you will look like a white person," to which I replied, "I like being black."

My mother was always a voracious reader and lover of the arts. She took me to see theatre plays, ballet, concerts, exhibitions, gatherings and parties where there were always artists.

I remember seeing a staging of 'A Streetcar Named Desire' when I was about 11 years old and the director's face when my mother introduced me and I told him how much I liked it. Even when it was violent and sad, I loved the passion of the story.

At home I had many books. There were some beautifully illustrated ones, especially those of Russian origin. I spoke and understood Russian until I was about five years old. When I began trying to fit in, I asked my mother not to speak to me in Russian anymore, because I didn't want to understand and that's how I forgot it—trying to be a normal Cuban kid.

I liked to write stories and draw. Many times, I invented stories, which I used to read to my friends or I would just narrate while I was creating them. I was the storyteller for the little ones when I went to parties with my mother. The painting and drawing were also, for me, a way of telling stories, just in a different way. I remember singing but only to tell a story-song, because I never liked to sing in public.

The music I listened to from when I was two or three until I was ten or eleven years old was from the radio, TV shows, movies or on the turntable at home, until the 'Special Period'[35] when the turntable needles couldn't be obtained because the country was in economic crisis. One of my dreams when I was six

---

35   The Special Period in Time of Peace in Cuba was a time of economic crisis that began in 1991. It was the result of the dissolution of the Soviet Union and Cuba's dearth of trading partners, only easing slightly in the late 1990s when Venezuela became Cuba's main trading partner. There were shortages of fuel, food and services.

or seven years old was to hear a program where they only played my favourite songs. The music I remember from that time was—well, here is part of my playlist from then.

Beny Moré, Celina González, El Guayabero, Los Compadres, Trio Matamoros, Vieja trova Santiaguera, Arsenio Rodríguez, Orquesta Aragón, José Antonio Mendez, Elena Burque, María Teresa Vera, Pablo Milanés, José Luis Ferrer, Xiomara augart, Annia Linares, Afrocuba, Los Papines, Las congas de los Carnavales, Conjunto Son 14, Tina Turner, Nat King Cole, The Supremes, The Beatles, Maria Elena Walsh, Caetano Veloso, Ellis Regina, Joan Manuel Serrat, Ana Belén, Lola Flores, Gardel, Piotr Ilich Chaikovski, Ludwig Minkus, Chopin, Verdi and so many others. You will see a lot of Cuban artists as well as well-known ones.

When I was twelve, I began studying fine arts in a school where I shared the classroom with other students studying classical ballet and music. There I discovered abstractionism, the impressionists, pop art and that the fine artists were the ones questioning the system and institutions. I learned that music students were ready to joke in any circumstance and were more relaxed about life in general and how dancers dieted even in a country where being able to eat was a luxury. This the dark side of a school of art—along with the competition and the incompetence. I saw students who, from the time they entered with their personal plan or dream, had to sacrifice them due to criticism from teachers and classmates. I saw the expressions and ideas that were not part of the fashion of the moment had no space within the collective. On the other hand, there were also professors who taught me about common discourses between the arts, about great literature such as Borges[36] and Lezama (Jose Lezama Lima)[37] and how any material could be the starting point for a work of art. I thank Alexis Lago, Hanna Shomenko, Antonia Eiriz, Clarisa and Alejandrina Cue very much for what I am as a visual artist.

Around the age of fourteen, I started listening to bands like Nirvana, The Doors, Pearl Jam, Alanis Morissette, Annie Lennox, Sting, King Crimson,

---

36   Jorge Francisco Isidoro Luis Borges Acevedo was an Argentinian writer and translator, and a key figure in Spanish literature. His best-known books, *Ficciones* (Fictions) and *El Aleph* (The Aleph), published in the 1940s. Borges' works have contributed to philosophical literature and the fantasy genre, and have been considered by some critics to mark the beginning of the magic realist movement in 20th century Latin American literature.

37   Lezama (José Lezama Lima) was a Cuban writer and poet who is considered one of the most influential figures in Latin American literature

Jimmy Hendrix, Radiohead, Coldplay, Sintesis, Estado de Animo, Vanito Brown, El duo Cachivache, Carlos Varela, Bjork, Lorena Mcquenit, Enya, Gerardo Alfonso and X Alfonso and it was at this stage that I began to compose. The first song was called 'Around Around' and the words went like this:

Around Around
Life goes around
A hand in the air
Something to cry
Your smile is my condition
And your body is my fiction
For this I say
Life goes around
Around Around.

At that time, I spoke almost no English but suddenly I had ideas in English, and understood the meaning of some phrases. Of course, for me these sketches of songs that I hummed or sang and called my 'ghosts' were nothing more than ideas of a musical world to which I did not belong.

When I was fifteen, I started to study for a bachelor certificate in a school that wasn't the one I wanted. It was assumed I would go to the fine art school to continue my artistic education, but that year I learned that sometimes talent is not the way to get a place in life. You need to know the right people or you are out. So, I was unable to get into the school I wanted. I was very upset when I found out. My mother went to speak with the director and he told her (to her face) that I had some of the best qualifications, but I wasn't recommended by an important person so…. My mother tried to look for a person who could support me and she finally found someone, but then I said I didn't want to be in a school where they didn't value talent. So, my school was in the city, unlike like most of the bachelor schools in Havana which were boarding schools and further away.

These schools were not nice because it was like being in jail for many of the people I knew that went to them. The idea of those schools or *Becas* was that students could work and study, but there was a lot of pressure because of the bullying by the students and sometimes the teachers. They didn't have much food and they couldn't see their family for a week or sometimes two.

So, it turned out I was lucky not to get in and went to a school where many of the 'red *bourgeois* children' went. These were the children of the military and diplomats who were the ruling class. I saw the reality of the only ruling party—the military—and Fidel had it all. People, like my family and the family of some of my friends—well, we were just numbers. My granddad fought with Fidel in the Sierra Maestra (a mountain range in Cuba) and he raised us to believe in a Cuban revolution as being best for Cuba, but I saw there that it was fake and an illusion.

I remember the comments of some of those students, the children of the military, talking about spending twice the monthly salary of a normal citizen at a disco. It was like living with people from another reality.

That was in 1994—a time in Cuba where the economy was so bad that having food was a privilege for some people. I was the little one of the house, so my family used to leave me the best food to eat. I used to walk everywhere most of the time because the transport was awful. The journey from my house to the school was very long and I used to spend a lot of time walking or I might try to hitchhike.[38]

I realized I needed to earn some money to help so I went to one of the big editorials in Havana with all my drawings in a roll and I asked to speak with the designer. He was a lovely person called Montoto and he gave me my first job as illustrator and more work after that.

Were there personal changes or events which affected the direction you and your music took? Can you tell me some of these?

AA: When I was about eighteen, after I finished school, I had a personal and family crisis. My granddad died, my first love emigrated to Spain and I was feeling so lonely in Havana because many friends were leaving Cuba as well. It took me two years to recover and I was crying most of the time. Music was the way I used to release that pain. I had a guitar that my ex-boyfriend gave me and I started learning alone while composing.

I met Gonzalo Rubalcaba through my sister's family and heard his music. At

---

38   Here Arema shows me a map showing a marked route from her house to the school. It is just under 12 km.

the age of nineteen, I went to a jazz festival in Havana, where I rediscovered Chucho Valdés and met Bobby Carcasses. I remember seeing Roy Hargrove and his band playing. I was backstage with a friend of his and they were completely super happy. It was as if nothing mattered and at the same time, they gave everything. I liked that feeling very much.

That year was when I started music school. I enrolled in an evening school for adults because I overheard a neighbour shouting at her daughter about the entrance exam so I asked them about the course. Even though I never saw myself singing and was really more interested in composition, the only option I had was the singing programme.

In the program I learned how to write music and that opened the door to getting in contact with other people who might sing or play my music. I started writing as soon as I could. Even when I had a few pieces played by friends or sung by the choir I realized that I could develop my work, so I decided to start singing.

I went to a place in Havana called *El Caserón del Tango* and sang so quietly that only the people in front of me could hear.

While all this was happening, I was working as an illustrator for magazines and books and with a hip-hop group writing and helping them to work with their vocals. I remember what some of the hip-hop people said to me. They said, 'Oh you are good, you write like a man.'

Although I was writing for male performers, they didn't say it because of my approach. It was their way of saying they liked my way of writing. To be a girl in a hip-hop world was hard. You needed to be strong in order to be noticed and respected. Thanks to my approach to hip-hop I learned a bit about RnB soul music. I was influenced by groups and artists including The Refugees, Jill Scott, Busta Rhymes (rapper), 2Pac and Mos Def. I found these very interesting.

While I was at the music school composing a choral piece that was a conga for ten voices I was also listening to Debussy, Yma Sumac, Bach, Gershwin, Astor Piazzolla and others.

In that time, I got Involved with a magazine called *La Isla Infinita* and they decided to work with a group of musicians on a Medieval play. I was one of a group of artists making the props and I created a poem to invite the people to come and see the play. It was called 'The Speech of Harlequin' and it felt like the Renaissance spirit.

That magazine was well known to academics so my work as an illustrator gained me recognition but I felt divided between music and painting. People from either side would say to me, "leave the painting, you can create good music". Or, "forget the music, you have a career as a painter and illustrator." But really, I was both.

During a hip-hop festival in Havana, when I was trying to show a piece that was choral/ hip hop and jazz to one of the hip-hop artists I knew (even though he didn't really understand my idea), a man behind me interrupted me. I was afraid that he was trying to flirt with me so I didn't really look at him. He said that he liked the musical idea I was showing and invited me to a meeting. I didn't go, but a few years later I discovered he was Ivan Berry.[39]

Are there any particular people you remember who helped you in music?

AA: I will always be thankful to my two singing professors: Olga Diaz who helped me enter into the music school after listening to one of my songs. Apparently she said, "I want to have this student in my class or I won't start the semester!" She was so supportive and this was surprising because she didn't know me at all. She thought that I would become a *Bel Canto* singer, but that wasn't my calling.

Miguel was a teacher who helped me find my voice. He used to tell me: "To sing well, means to let the notes come out effortlessly, as if the notes and you are floating". He used to charge very little for his classes, because he wanted even students with almost no money, to have the possibility to learn.

Later, the three professors that helped me a lot to develop my musical ideas were firstly Rosario, my guitar professor who taught me as an extra-curricular activity because I wasn't allowed to be studying both guitar and singing at the

---

39   Ivan Berry started the *BeatFactory* in 1982. *BeatFactory* provided a launching ground for many of urban music's successful artists. Berry later headed up A and R for and International for Sony BMG Canada f2000-2004, He was influential in the careers of artists including Wyclef, Sloan, Rascalz, Treble Charger, In Essence, and many more. He is actively involved in music across the Caribbean and is in demand across the globe as speaker and guest at different events.

music school. She used to teach me at her home. She had a cheerful, strong spirit and introduced me to "Les Luthiers" (an Argentinian musical comedy group) and to Leo Brower music, which has the beauty of the rhythm and edgy harmonies and many other composers. We share the same love for *La Trova, El Filin* and the amazing Marta Valdés. She said to me once "Say 'Yes' until you have the need to say 'No', open yourself to the opportunities". That was very useful advice for my life in general and also as a performer.

The other one is Enerlo Lisa. She gave pearls of wisdom in every class. She had very interesting insights about music and she taught me to listen carefully, to see the music as a sound-scape in front of me, about its diversity. She taught me that creators pushing boundaries take risks, and that it is important to be a believer and a searcher. I loved her classes.

The classes with the Maestro Guerrero were a very special gift. He was a well-known composer and orchestral director and I was lucky to be in some of his classes for young composers. He used to ask us to develop music ideas and then he analyzed them with us. He used to say "You may learn to analyze many things, but what really knows is your heart and there is no explanation". He was an enigmatic person, but also very fun and full of life.

So, where did you go from there?

I couldn't continue my classes because when I was twenty-three, I give birth to my eldest son it was very hard time for me. I switched to survival mode. I lived for two years with the father of my son but after that he was often not present. I worked as a street vendor, selling bakery products, initially carrying my baby with me (because private business was illegal in Cuba). My grandmother was living with me and according to her I was wrong to work for myself. She was a believer in the revolution—but that didn't pay for food.

When my son was three years old, I decided to go back to music and also continue my work as an illustrator. I knew I needed to stop selling cakes in the street. That wasn't me. It was just a temporary situation. I started playing my guitar and singing in public, most of the time for free. After I played, I felt very strong. The lives of my son and grandmother were in my hands, so I decided to work out a way to make a living from music.

I met Moises, a friend who help me record some of my songs in his home studio. He is also the co composer of Mal, the last song on the *Red Soundtracks*. Most of the work we recorded in his studio was lost, because back then I didn't have a hard drive or a computer to save my work and his computer crashed and we lost all our work. He is one of few friends that from the beginning, believed and supported my ideas of blending genres and experimenting.

In 2008 I went to Italy to a Cuban festival in Milan. After a concert I did at *Smeraldo Theatre*, a friend of the director told me that he would tell his brother (a record label owner) about me. Days after that, the director of the festival took me to me one of the heads of *Schema Records*, introducing herself as my manager. I did not even speak Italian but I understood they wanted me to record with them. The director said she would arrange a formal meeting. However, the date they asked for a meeting was the same day I was due to fly back to Cuba. I had no money to change my flight and no power to do so even if I had because as a Cuban citizen you were not allowed to ask to extend your visa. So, I end up returning to Cuba with no Internet to communicate with the *Schema Records* people.

One day I was in the Plaza de Armas, in Havana, where a group of friends and I gathered to rehearse and in the distance was Sting and his wife Trudie walking with a group of people. I always loved Sting's music and so did my friend Yolexys who played the guitar with me. So, we went and we spoke with them and played one song for him. We didn't want to stress him and the woman of the Ministry of Culture who was with them was continually saying, 'they need to go to sleep.' (She was a bit annoying really). But Sting, his wife and friends were very happy to see us playing. I didn't have a phone number or any contact so we just left saying, 'thank you' to them. One of the artists who was there gave me a photograph and told me that that Sting really liked us.

One day visiting a friend in his studio I met a composer and producer called Juan Antonio Leyva and he listened to one of my songs and asked me to go to a casting of a film that he was music producer for. I went, but I didn't pass the casting. He said, "That's impossible, I was the one selecting the musical cast!" The film, 'Habana Blues' was about the underground music in Havana and musicians like me that were creating a new wave of Cuban art. After that day we started collaborating and I also met his wife Taby who is also a producer and composer. We worked for TV shows and films until I left Cuba. I really miss them because I used to share my music with them as I created it.

I got involved in a project called the *Havana Cultura* project and there I met Gilles Peterson thanks to François Renié who was behind the project. I am very grateful for the introduction to Gilles because that project and the resulting album opened many doors for my music and also for many musicians like me in Cuba.

You now live in Barcelona—how did you come to live there?

AA: I came to Barcelona through an invitation to play in a festival. The person who invited me was a Cuban woman, the sister of a friend. When I met her in Cuba, I told her I wasn't interested on going anywhere unless the conditions were good because I was finding my way within the Cuban scene. She said, 'of course', but in the end she didn't pay for my flights, after she arranged the whole journey and I was obliged to play. In Cuba it's very difficult to get a visa and she sent me all the information to apply for one but when I got it, she told me, I'm sorry I don't have money to pay for your flights'. However, a friend who wanted me to play in France paid for my flights. So, I told her I had the tickets to go and to do the concerts. Even so, she wasn't at the airport when I arrived. Yet thanks to the Energy four a friend gave me a contact of a photographer, Jaume Peracaula, who used to work in a film school in Cuba and he give me a room in his house as well as a lot of advice about things I had yet to learn about life in Barcelona. That was an amazing blessing.

I was in a situation where I needed to fulfill my commitment with my friend and the concert in France but I was in Barcelona and even though I was grateful to Jaume I knew I couldn't stay any longer in his house. He helped me by calling the woman that invited me and she said that now she didn't have anything for me, but I could work as career for her mother in law. I said, 'I'm sorry but you are going to introduce me to the festival and the music scene here because I need to survive until I go to play in France and it is what we agreed'. I met two musicians and one of them allowed me to live in his house while we were playing together and helped me out. I was distressed and when I wasn't playing, I stayed in the house all the time. Then one day I received an invitation to a jam. The director of an Afrobeat band invited me to join them. I was very sad thinking about all that was happening but finally I went thanks to the musician that was working with me. He said, 'Go out, play your music!!' There I met Dany, the man who would become my husband. Many things happened afterwards before we got married.

So, after a month in Barcelona I decided to go to Italy en route to France and one of the things that I did was to meet Luciano Cantone and Davide from *Schema Records* and I told them what had happened before. We had a meeting and it was good. However, I was worried about my visa status so I contacted the office of an institution in Cuba. They said they would take care of my visa if I paid a big percentage of my contract to them. I sent them all my information and thought they were doing the paper work for the visa. However, when I went to my consulate in Milan the consul told me that my visa was expired. I never received anything from the institution. I was now illegally in Europe and if I flew to Cuba, I could not return to Europe for ten years.

The implication of this resounded deeply in me because my son was in Cuba with my grandmother I had so many things going on. I was recording with *Schema Records* and also on *Havana Cultura* records back in Cuba. I had concerts coming up too. The Consul said the best thing to do was go to Spain because if I stayed in Italy, I might end up in a deportation camp. I knew these were not nice places. My life at that moment felt like it was going down a hole.

One moment I was believing I could come and go from Cuba like a normal free citizen, see my son, work internationally, be with the man I loved and the next, I was told I had overstayed my visa. I was now in Barcelona, but illegally.

I managed to play in France a few times, but I couldn't go on a plane. This meant I could not tour with the *Havana Cultura Band*. My son was in Cuba so Dany and I, who were now living together, decided to bring him out to live with us and we did everything we could to make that happen. I was babysitting because that was the only work I could get without papers. I also played concerts when I could. Dany was working as an actor with a theatre company, as well as doing voiceovers. I got pregnant and although I wasn't in the mood for having another baby his words convinced me. He is such a lovely human being. He said that this child was a blessing for him so I ended up having my second baby. That was marvelous. We married in a little town filled with rosemary and thyme, surrounded by close friends. When our baby was a year old, we went to Cuba on a thirty-hour journey flying from Barcelona to Moscow and then Havana because it was cheaper—we had little money even to pay our rent and there was a lot of cost in paperwork.

Finally, after three months there, we made it and brought our older son back to Barcelona with us. It was a military operation, ruled by a very specific schedule of expiring documents, but well worth it.

In 2016 when Dany had a big voice-over job, he asked me what I would like and I told him 'Native Instruments and Ableton Live (software) to create demos to show my ideas to musicians' and he bought them for me. I didn't know how to use them but I sat down and started creating until I learned simply by doing it. This is how the 'The Red Soundtracks' was made—while I was learning how to use those programs and I am still learning every day.

What would you say was the 'essence' of your music—how might you describe your music to someone else?

AA: My music as see it is always a mix, it's mostly visual. I am interested in the emotion and the story that the songs contain. I don't really care about genres; they are tools to express the feelings and to place the characters. My way of thinking is mostly cinematic when I listen to music. I need to visualize where it's placed, what is happening and I need to believe it, to get into it, to enjoy it.

Is there something special about jazz for you? You talk about people you listened to who influenced you like Ella but what draws you to jazz?

AA: I like jazz because it's not one thing. Jazz has many genres within itself. It represents freedom and I love it when I can walk at the edges.

You are involved in painting, visual arts, fashion and music. How do you relate these areas?

AA: I would love to be able to continue creating music painting filming and connecting all the art work as one in a binding project.

You are a mother and when we have spoken in the past you have been breathlessly haring up a hill on your way to collect your children from school. How do you fit being a mother in with your ambitions in music? Would you say being a mother means you bring a different element to the music?

AA:: Being a mother is good because it gives you focus and you need a lot of will to get things done, but at the same time if you don't have support, it consumes a lot of time so you cannot be as present in the music scene as before. Shows you do may be late at night or far away and if you have a lot of gigs in a row you are going to maybe be away for days and this is not good if you have little ones. I think that for every person life can be taken in different ways, for some it's easier to be moving and for others it can be difficult.

How do you see the future of women in music—do you feel they are respected now as equals and do you see their roles changing?

AA: I saw a change in the 90's. It was like an explosion of powerful women, speaking up for their rights, singing and talking about their world, from their point of view, not wanting to be what was expected of them. This is still happening. We are still standing up. The industry tries to sell women like dolls and tries to close the door to the ones that don't represent this 'cute babe' image, but also more and more independent artists are gaining space and their way of presenting themselves is wider and more diverse, which is good because art is a reflection of the world, so it needs to be diverse.

If you could offer advice to a younger you, or a young woman just entering the music industry, what would that be?

AA: My personal advice to all the artists is to keep experimenting and to try to maintain their freedom by deciding for themselves what they are doing, so they can really channel the Creative Energy. For anybody to find their personal way it's necessary to walk a different path and to learn about their own relationship with the world. An artist can have different faces and outcomes, because it is good to get in contact with different things. I would advise, do collaborations, change formats. It's good to feel happy with your work, even the unfinished, the not so good, because you can learn from everything.

I have known people that share and offer guidance, but in general, it's not as often as it could be. It's such a competitive world that for many they only can see a door for themselves to pass through and after that, some even close it to feel that they are safe. I am used to sharing information all the time and I love creating connections where people can meet and create. I am not expecting others to do it or to be obliged to do it, but it is just so they can return what I have given them. I really believe in Energy[40] and I think that when one opens a door to help others, that helpful Energy will come back when it is needed. So my main advice would be to be persistent, focused, to be true to yourself. Defend your ideas, while at the same time, be aware of the signs and advice that life offers. Learn from every experience, because our journey is a lesson. Share your light with good people, and wish and do well by others in every instance, because there is always a way for those who pursue a dream.

Barb Jungr

"Creativity is one of those overused words, like spirituality, but at its core it is a deep running river. Creativity frees the mind, and spirit. It is the point of it all."

Barb Jungr is a stalwart supporter of music and musicians. She brings with her an energy and positivity which she shares. I was Barb's guest at a gig a couple of years ago and during the interval I got talking to a couple of women. It turned out they had been to see Barb eight times and were massive fans. During the break, they spotted me and came over to say 'hello'. I told her about the ladies that had sat next to me. Next thing I knew I was squished up a bit, Barb sat between me and the ladies and her attention was fully on these women, asking them how far they had come and thanking them for supporting her. She only left when she realized she had to go to the loo, get changed and had about five minutes before the second part of the show began. She told me I was to stay and meet some people with her afterwards. Two grinning women sat next to me now. Barb does that for people. Her personality, charisma and strength are amazing—as is her talent for narrative vocals. She seems interested in everything, from Mongolian nomadic throat singing tapes someone sent her to her love of finding new words—and she particularly seems to like those with several meanings.

Even though she is busy Barb will try to make time for a chat because she is interested life and people. I have interviewed Barb in the past and learned that she comes from Rochdale in northern England and grew up in Stockport. Her parents were Czech/German and as a child she was part of what she described

---

40   Energy is something Arema believes in- a force surrounding us which give positivity and connections.

to me as 'a refugee family among Irish Catholics who were absorbed and made welcome'. In the mid-1950s in the UK when Barb was growing up, many families did not yet have TV so as a small child, Barb used to turn the front step of the family's terraced home in Rochdale into a stage and perform shows with her dolls.

Her father said it was hard to shut Barb up and she had the ability to recall tunes she heard just a couple of times on the radio and sing them. A student of the violin from age seven to fifteen, Barb was given solo slots at music festivals. When she was a teenager, she formed a folk group called Arwen with school friends and sang their songs around Manchester. She studied botany at Leeds University and everywhere she went, Barb joined jazz bands, folk groups and sang wherever she could.

At *Goldsmiths* in London she studied for a master in ethnomusicology and became immersed in the world of punk music and alternative cabaret. She also briefly held a post writing for The Singer magazine before it went under. In 1982 Barb and her harmony group the *Three Courgettes* had a top 100 hit with their theme song (*The Three Courgettes*, Island Records 1982) which was released in three different versions. That year, she also toured with Kid Creole and The Coconuts.

It is Barb's unique take on narrative songs like those of Bob Dylan, Leonard Cohen and Bob Brel that have gained her most critical acclaim, but she has also written her own material and sung the music of David Bowie, Joni Mitchell, Stephen Sondheim and many others. She performs largely as a solo artist but also with other musicians including Ian Shaw, Claire Martin, Christine Collister and Michael Parker and has had a long association with Julian Clary. So, interviewing Barb I knew I would get forthright, honest answers. I was right and Barb talks about the industry, the process of writing, education and much more.

The Barb Jungr Interview

Who were your early influences, not just in music (though these would be great to talk about) but on you as a person?

BJ: Not so much people as things. One of my biggest influences was the vinyl recording we had of the musical South Pacific. The music, the pictures on the record sleeve, the story. I was captivated and lived inside it all. So, Rodgers and Hammerstein were right there. Theatre and cinema were huge for me.

We were in a small community in Rochdale. It was a working class—cobbled streets, front opening for coal to be thrown in, the lot. The Catholic Church was the centre of it, and they had local—we'd call them 'am dram' now but that word wouldn't have existed then—theatre productions. They staged loads of things, and we went to see them as well as everything in Manchester including (even though I was little) opera and films alongside pantomime. My Aunty Nora, who was not my aunt but the lady who looked after me while my mum was working, was a huge influence.

I am curious Barb. In your music, you often take songs of well-known writers like Dylan, Cohen, Brel, The Beatles, Sting and others and re-interpret them. Does this happen as a conscious decision? Do you seek out songs or is it more a case of when you hear a song your mind says, 'Wow, I could do that there, or change that just a little bit'. How does it happen?

BJ: I never think of what I might or might not do, I just start with the song knocking on my door and shouting in my ear and then we—whoever I am working with—sit at the piano and sing it and play it and see if there's anything coming down to help us, any new way into the song. It's all from the gut. I don't really do anything cerebrally, it's pretty much always intuition. The cerebral stuff comes after, in the arranging and so on but the process at root and then in performance must, for me, always have as far as possible an absence of thought and be utterly instinctive. Songs catch me like a butterfly in a net. I don't know that is going to happen. And there's such a lot that lives in the air, in the area of "hope". I hope it's going to work; I hope I can bring something to the song, and the song can grow somewhere with me. None of it is a given. It's magical.

You have been involved with education and written for children's and musical theatre. What drew you to that? How do children react to your works? Over all, how does this part of your work feel?

BJ: I stopped teaching in institutions many years ago now. I found it too distracting from performance and writing but I do master class work and private consultation, which I enjoy a great deal. I write quite a lot these days and work in theatre which I enjoy enormously. I love the creation of new musicals for children and adults and I am very lucky to have a group of creative collaborators and theatres who are very supportive of my work. This is all music, it is all performance, it is all arranging. It is all worlds and lyrics and tunes. There's no separation for me of one from another. They all play alongside each other quite happily. It is a change of head space sometimes but that is beautiful and encourages directional changes in thought processes. I think creativity is a river, and if you give it room to flow, you have no idea where it will lead. You have to jump in and swim. There's a lot of trust involved.

Your mother and father were from two different cultures—did this affect the influences you drew on at first or later?

BJ: I think it's had a massive effect on my outlook and being in the world and I'm really happy about it. And it brought into my genetic fabric a love for a lot of things musically that I might not have found otherwise.

I remember you told me, as a child you would perform on your doorstep even to friends. Was yours a household where you felt you could express yourself? Were you encouraged to be creative?

BJ: Oh no. I just was going my own way, always. My parents were a bit baffled I think by me, but they became my biggest fans in the end. I think it was good that I wasn't given everything because I had to fight inside and outside myself to do what I ended up doing and I think that's a good thing. I live in a constant cloud of doubt but again, I think that's good because it forces you to move forward. I think if everything is easy that can work either way. On the other hand, yesterday, I met a young actor who is fast becoming a star and he has just landed onto the slide of life with everything working for him and total support and he's doing great. It's about the kind of people we are, I guess. There are no rules in anything in the arts, in my book. Everything is up for grabs, always. My father-in-law—I am no longer married and my ex is long gone and also long dead, but I have only ever had the one father-in-law and we have remained family. He is Frank Bowling and is a painter of considerable renown. We were talking (about my ex and life and so on) and he said something which deeply resonated with me, which was that all he wants is to go to the studio and paint something better than he painted the day before. And I think that sums up my own feeling about playing live, about recording, about writing, about it all. What I want is to do better than I did before. For myself. That's my personal standard and goal. It is internal, not external. And I think that's always been somewhere in there.

Your career has been incredibly diverse from singing in Portobello market with the Three Courgettes, to touring with Kid Creole, Sade, The Jets, Mari Wilson, cabaret and jazz. Is there anyone area you really love and feel more at home in than others?

BJ: Music is music and performing is performing and singing is singing and writing is writing. They all feed into one another and I love them all. They are all equally adored! But I've been incredibly lucky to have moved through all kinds of genres and situations and collaborations and I've learned so much from them all. Those days with *The Three Courgettes* were so innocent, but we did so much and had so much fun doing it. The tours I did with Julian Clary remain deeply in my heart. The years of shows alongside Mari Wilson and Claire Martin in *Girl Talk* were a total blast. Working with Mark Anthony Turnage blew my mind harmonically, as did collaborating with Laurence Hobgood.

Your work with young people is well known, from coaching young offenders, teaching voice to university students. How do you see the future for them and music? Are they interested and do they engage with music?

BJ: I do very little teaching these days. I get asked to coach at professional level and master class work and I like that but I have little desire to be in mainstream education. I think it is marvelous that musicians can earn their living doing other things because we have been SO badly let down by the music industry that to earn a living from playing music and recording music itself has been pretty much demolished except at the level of major "pop" celebrities. My concern is we turn people into a world where they cannot earn their living from the making of music. But the people coming out of conservatoires and colleges are of huge talent and the infrastructure of support for them to go out and play and learn is badly deteriorated. But phoenixes do rise out of ashes and pendulums swing. Somehow, I am hopeful again that they will invigorate everything with their enthusiasm and joy. People do still come to hear live music and people still run tiny clubs at vast expense to their own sanity (particularly in jazz). So I remain optimistic for music and musicians, but absolutely livid with the music industry who have betrayed working musicians.

You also work with local people on creative projects—can you explain one or two of these and also say why you feel this is important if you do?

BJ: I love working with professional and local projects because you see and feel the difference in people when they are engaged and asked to reach new levels of expertise. I worked for several years as Artistic Director of *Deep Roots Tall Trees* in Corby, a project I originated with cultural engineer and local heroine Rosalind Stoddart. We were very lucky to receive, both from local benefactors and the Arts Council, funding to come into being and making pieces which included local songwriters and a choir, all mentored by professionals. We staged several hugely successful pieces, one with the London Philharmonic Orchestra, in a football ground in Corby with songs and writers together and arranged with them playing! Imagine! That was stratospheric for the people involved. And a core group of people formed not only firm friendships but allegiances that took them to experiencing all manner of performances and participation. I saw first-hand the changes those events and experiences provoked and the resulting joy and expansion of horizons people enjoyed. Creativity is one of those overused words, like spirituality, but at its core it is a deep running river. Creativity frees the mind, and spirit. It is the point of it all.

As a woman, how have you found your journey through the music industry? With jazz in particular what are the key changes you have noticed if any?

I wish I could say I thought things were tons better, I really do. But you can still count on one hand the number of jazz DJs and writers who are women and this will not change until the people who run stations and edit magazines hire more women to write and edit and onto boards for festivals etc. etc. I think there's improvement but its snail paced. There are more women musicians which is great, but it's in the fabric of the jazz world we need more and more. I am less kind these days as I get older about the nonsense women have to put up with which is often unchallenged because who wants to lose work? So, we have nonsense from all kinds of quarters and we do our smiling and grimace and get on with it all. So, I have gotten on with it all and made my own career out of blood and sweat and some considerable help from my friends. And maybe in the arts that's the only way we can? I don't know anymore. I just get up and if I start feeling cross about the world and its ways I write and go to a rehearsal and get on with it. Sometimes my great singing female friends and I will just have a five-minute moan together, that's always, while useless practically, refreshing.

How has your work schedule affected your personal life? Do you find you have time to see family/friends?

I think you have to recognize that if you are a gigging musician you are always going to miss out on things that happen for most other people at weekends and in evenings. My family and friends are wise now to it and so they give me tons of time ahead and if something's super important I will block it out in my diary so it doesn't get booked; but then there are the things that come from left field and you have to say, "yes" to them. But I think people who love you understand that music is life and if you make music it is always going to be a priority because it's a vocation and not a career and that is *so* true of jazz. You do it because you want to and you must. People learn to live with that but I suspect that's also why a lot of musicians hang with other musicians. And you always make time for the people you love. I have female friends—musicians—who have brought up families while gigging perfectly well. Their children are pretty amazingly adjusted, as it happens. And all of them also play!

If you were to meet your younger self, just contemplating a career in music, is there any advice you would offer?

BJ: I would begin with: "Have you thought of being a lawyer? They have big houses and make loads of dosh and have gardens and holidays". Then I would fall about laughing and say, "Go girl, sing and write. Sing and write like a bloody maniac, because that's what you're born to do".

♭ ♭ ♭

Georgia Mancio

"I never take for granted the symbiotic relationship between audience and artist and in increasingly dystopian times, I feel the nurturing of dialogue, empathy and acceptance are more pressing than ever."

"What jazz means to me—and how I choose to interpret it—will never be the same as for anyone else. It allows you to find and be yourself and then develop that self beyond your expectations and comfort zones."

Georgia Mancio is a vocalist and recording artist. She is curator of the annual *Hang* events in London where she gathers musicians from across Europe and the World to perform as a residency. Hugely talented herself she has performed and collaborated with many musicians on the UK jazz scene and recorded with Kate Williams (daughter of guitarist John Williams). Georgia and I met at a pub local to a hotel where I was staying. On hearing the hotel name Georgia said, 'Oooh, the musicians' hotel!' It turned out the St. Giles hotel in London was where many of the musicians she gathered together for one of her *Hang* events stayed, so she knew it well. She is also great company, a musician who believes in the power of music and enjoys a cheeky half of Guinness on occasion (or two). Georgia tells of her love of jazz music, curating major events, bereavement and the positive future of jazz and music. I have seen her perform and she has this amazing presence on stage, people can't take their eyes off of her and she sings with style and grace. She also occasionally replaces her vocals with lines of perfectly pitched whistling and her scat singing is really good, a skill which only a few have, Georgia being one of them.

The Georgia Mancio Interview

Who would you say influenced your early life—not just in music but you as a person?

GM: I was born in the UK but brought up bilingual, speaking both Italian and English. My cultural reference points were also very split which of course I didn't appreciate as a child, desperate to fit in with my peers. Now I realize I was very fortunate to have been surrounded by art, languages and a broader outlook and that sense of being different, a misfit, an outsider is actually pretty good preparation for life as an artist!

My parents both came to the UK (separately) from Italy for different reasons then met and built a life in London. Maybe because they were starting again from scratch, they had a very strong work ethic and both embraced life in a new country whilst maintaining their own cultural heritage and links.

My dad was a talented photographer and artist but having seen his parents struggle to raise a family as professional musicians, he chose a more secure route. I think not working in a creative environment compromised him spiritually although he sustained a passionate relationship with the arts, from listening to Beethoven, Mahler or Liszt every morning, to painting, even to the way he dressed and how he styled our home.

When I was about ten, he bought Frank Sinatra's 'Only the Lonely' and a box set of jazz records. It was like a light going on for me! I learnt every word and, without knowing who I was listening to or their significance, discovered Louis Armstrong, Betty Carter, Lambert Hendricks and Ross (an American vocalese trio), Anita O'Day, Carmen McRae, Abbey Lincoln and many more. It sowed a seed very deep for my future, even though it took me a long time to actually grow it.

My mum was an incredibly vivacious and dynamic person, fiercely loyal and fair. She believed in peace, freedom and equality for all human beings: lessons that certainly imprinted and became very important to me in life and work. She showed me what it means to be passionate and dedicated to your work. Teaching Italian language and literature was her true vocation. The classroom was her stage and I remember my sister and myself, sometimes sitting at the back of her classes, watching her hold her students spellbound in a mixture of devotion and a little fear!

My sister, though only three years older, was both a third parent in my childhood and closest ally. Never wanting to miss out on what she was doing meant I was reading books and plays (which we also acted out) ahead of my age and even if I didn't fully understand, I was hooked on the seemingly endless world of stories and storytelling out there.

Why jazz singing? Can you describe how singing makes you feel, what you like about it, the sounds or anything else?

GM: I came to singing late because I held music in such reverence and didn't dare imagine it was something I could actually do. My paternal grandparents were classical musicians (they were both pianists and my grandmother also a singer) and impressed upon me the importance to take your time with music, particularly singing. I was never confident in a conventional learning space so it really took time to find the right teachers—or for them to find me and know how to nudge me in the right direction.

Singing is incredibly exposing: there are no buttons to press, not much to stand behind. You are involved physically, emotionally and spiritually. It is both internalized and externalized, sonically and intellectually, perhaps even more so with improvised music as you both plan what to sing next and react to the musicians you're playing with. You are constantly judging how far to push the boundaries, without compromising the story of the song.

What I love most about practicing jazz singing is how personal that judgment is. What jazz means to me—and how I choose to interpret it—will never be the same as for anyone else. It allows you to find and be yourself and then develop that self beyond your expectations and comfort zones. The notion of coming to a song fresh every time is daunting perhaps but also incredibly liberating. Like life itself, there are multiple routes to navigate: some will be smooth, others will derail you but you have to learn how to handle and love the surprises.

How do you feel about young people and jazz? Do you feel there is still the interest there was a few years ago or is this growing? Do you think education is making a difference?

GM: I am based in the UK and it's very heartening and exciting to see more young people embracing this art form than ever before—mainly as students and practitioners but things are changing (certainly in London) with younger audience members too, which we have really needed for some time.

I think formalized jazz education has had a huge impact and the standard is incredibly high. It's important to remember though that you cannot learn everything in the classroom. Jazz is something to be experienced on the road, in front of all kinds of audiences, with all types of musicians, of all ages. Mostly you need to find your own truth, your own story and personality and that doesn't—and shouldn't—happen within the three or four years of higher education. It takes a lifetime of nurturing, persistence, devotion, stubbornness and willpower!

Tell me about Hang. Why did you decide to organize the events and how do you find people to include?

GM: For five consecutive years (2010-2014) I ran an international voice festival called *ReVoice!* in association with the *Pizza Express Jazz Club* in London. Over the life of the festival I presented over 160 artists expanding from a five-night event to twelve nights across four venues both in and out of London. Apart from a couple of interns in the last two editions, I did everything on my own. What set the festival apart was that alongside curating, producing and presenting, I also performed forty-four sets myself, so I always met the artists I engaged as a fellow artist, not solely as a promoter. It was an enormous learning curve, more work than I would ever have imagined and I do sometimes wonder how I spun all those plates with very few breakages!

At the height of its popularity, I decided to take a step back, a decision which people still question five years on. I learnt as much from stopping as from creating it: that all paths are valid, they may just lead to a different destination and also the importance of being in charge of your own artistic destiny, not to be defined by the expectations or labeling of others. I surprised people: I surprised myself! Suddenly I had space to focus in again more fully on my own artistic output.

I have always liked working with different musicians in different contexts and opening up new collaborations. After the break I realized I wanted to bring these collaborations to the fore, whereas they had been support acts to *ReVoice!* artists. So *Hang* was born and each of the three editions I've produced so far (2017—2019) have found their own direction and flavour. For the most recent edition I presented my three current writing collaborations which was a landmark for me: 'Songbook' with pianist/composer Alan Broadbent, 'Finding Home' with pianist/composer/arranger Kate Williams and her septet and 'Where We Once Belonged'—a song cycle with pianist/songwriter Tom Cawley.

'ReVoice' and 'Hang' have allowed me to understand all aspects of the business, both on stage and behind the scenes—something I think all artists should experience and appreciate. I have also learnt to really trust my instincts about my artistic direction and fully commit to the project in front of me, despite the inevitable stress that comes with producing events.

Have you ever heard someone play and been totally blown away by what you are hearing?

There are a few performances that I hope will stay with me forever. The first was hearing Betty Carter when I worked as a waitress at Ronnie Scott's club over twenty years ago. At that time, I was studying film making. The notion of becoming a professional jazz singer was just a dream for me then so I couldn't fully appreciate the depth of her talent but the reaction to her music making and stage presence was so strong and visceral, I can summon those feelings instantly today.

When I produced *ReVoice!* the Norwegian artist/band *Beady Belle* took their already incredible performance to a stratospheric level on their encore. I have never seen any other performer do that: to bravely leave something behind just for that moment. Everything came together: technical virtuosity and a quasi-spiritual commitment to serving the music.

Other artists I will never forget are 'Little' Jimmy Scott and Andy Bey, who draw you into their utterly unique sound worlds and hold you there for years after! And *Sangam*, a trio with Charles Lloyd, Zakir Hussain and Eric Harland that was the most seamlessly integrated I've ever seen.

Finally, Sheila Jordan blew me (and everyone else there) away on her ninetieth birthday gig last year in London. A ninety-minute duo set with bassist Cameron Brown, followed by a sixty-minute set that she only curtailed because she announced, pointing to her partner, "he's tired!" To put it in context they had flown in from the US less than a week before and that morning from mainland Europe where they had played the previous night. Sheila brings such warmth, humanity and pure dedication to every performance and an undiminished desire to spread the word of this precious art form throughout the world. I am very fortunate to have become friends with her in the last ten years and know that she is a mentor and inspiration to many of us. People often ask what your ambitions are: mine is to stay as in love with this music as Sheila has and to know the greatest achievement is simply in keeping going.

Are there other events in your personal life which have affected your music? Do you think going through major events in life are useful/

good for musicians or do they make you close down emotionally?

GM: I think if you're seeking to be a truthful artist it is impossible not to be affected by life events—good and bad. I've become better at channeling the energy of trauma into performance and making it work and mostly find it very cathartic, but when I was younger and less confident about my identity and purpose as an artist, I was more easily overwhelmed.

My father's death in 2013 had a huge impact on me but the gift was a deeper connection to the music and the catalyst to my career as a lyricist. I had written here and there over the years but never with real focus or as a priority. In 2013 I had started playing with the double *Grammy*-winning pianist and composer, Alan Broadbent, and the following year, after a chance conversation, he sent me a beautiful song of his called 'The Long Goodbye' and asked if I would like to try writing a lyric. Bizarrely it coincided with what turned out to be the last visit to my dad's house which we had finally sold after many complications. The house became the protagonist of the new song 'The Last Goodbye' and led us to a songwriting collaboration, which five years on has resulted in over twenty-six co-written songs and two albums from our 'Songbook'.

Sadly, I find myself bereaved again as my mum died very unexpectedly just a few months ago. Honestly, I'm still working through the impact of losing a second parent but I know already it has forced another big shift in my outlook and no doubt next artistic statement. All I have learned about grieving is that it is an unpredictable, shape-shifting beast. I hope to be able to continue meeting it with courage and artistic growth but not at the expense of self-care.

Do you feel there a harder path for women in jazz music? Is this changing and do you see a future where gender will not be an issue?

I think it's still a harder path for women full stop. I do see positive change: many more women coming into the profession and many people sensitively finding a balance between giving an equal platform and not just tokenism. I've had the great support of male musicians, journalists and promoters, right from the start to my career until now so for the most part feel there is full acceptance.

But I am still staggered that some of the 'establishment' refuse to move with the times or even acknowledge the issues of under representation. It can be very awkward challenging these gatekeepers on a seemingly large and yet in reality small, inter-dependent scene.

Just last week after a concert, I asked a male reviewer if he would give the same critique (about reinterpreting jazz standards) to male instrumentalists that he had levied at me. He admitted he "probably wouldn't" yet proceeded to publish a review which was more about him than me, the musicians I was performing with or the female artists and writers I was paying a very personal tribute to that night.[41] He seemed proud to inform me (twice) that he had never previously heard of me, despite my twenty years as a professional, seven albums (all reviewed in the magazine for which he writes) and multiple nominations in national jazz awards.

I realized this was the power trip. Even when you continue to produce quality work, push boundaries, act professionally, maintain integrity, it can be diminished and so can you. It is upsetting but reaffirms the importance to keep on challenging all stereotypes and prejudices and supporting those looking to bring the future closer to the present.

If you could meet your younger self—just about thinking of a career in jazz music, is there any piece of advice you might give her?

GM: I know that if I could have looked ahead to the career I have now I would have been amazed and very proud. It's so easy to forget that living day to day, year to year, just keeping on keeping on. I would be stunned that someone who agonizes over what to order from a menu can now trust her instinct on important career changes and act on them with confidence.

So I would say: 'just make a start because you will never finish starting'. I would say that today's dreams are tomorrow's realities; that there is more time than you think and also a lot, lot less; that you'll never be good enough and yet you already are; that for every shadow there's a light and that if you don't find the way, it will find you.

---

41   Jazz Journal review of Georgia Mancio by Lean Knock published Nov 2019 https://jazzjournal.co.uk/2019/11/17/ljf-2019-georgia-mancio-open-the-door-a-celebration-of-female-artists/

Given a blank canvas, just Georgia looking at the world, what would you like to say to people who listen, come to gigs and buy your music?

Thank you. Thank you for your time, trust, attention, interaction, energy, openness, ideas, spirit, commitment and belief in the need for art in this world.

Without doubt being an artist is a personal quest to develop and challenge yourself, to reflect the world around you, to find your part in it but also the art of communication, of sharing, reaching, teaching, moving, is *paramount*. I never take for granted the symbiotic relationship between audience and artist and in increasingly dystopian times, I feel the nurturing of dialogue, empathy and acceptance are more pressing than ever.

Thank you for listening and being on this journey with me: I don't know where I'm going or when I'll get there but I know I need to keep travelling.

Julia Biel

"You are adventurers through emotional landscapes with me because we are all wandering and wondering souls searching the music for the answers to the questions we carry within. I want to say to all of you who have got in touch over the years or come to chat after a show, I never tire of hearing your reactions."

Julia Biel is the daughter of a Cape Town man who came to the UK after the apartheid regime destroyed his dreams of becoming a teacher. Soon after coming to England he met Julia's mother, who had grown up in the war-torn remains and poverty of post-World War II Germany. Julia took up the piano when she was five years old and she once told me, '*Whenever I would feel lost, I would find myself in the music and it has gradually become the touchstone of my existence.*'

Later, she met Idris Rahman (who would later become her life partner, producer and bass player) at Oxford and found amongst her musical loves, jazz. Moving to London she put together a home studio and found her own route through music. A member of the *F-IRE Collective* she made her first album with fellow members of the collective and co-wrote with guitarist Jonny Phillips. That album *Not Alone* won her a rising star nomination in the *BBC Jazz Awards* in 2006. Her next album *Love Letters & Other Missiles* came in 2015 and was nominated in the *MOBO* and *Urban Jazz Awards*. She has toured all over the world and her newest releases are solo works of just Julia and piano. I reviewed her recent release and it is superb.

The Julia Biel Interview

Who would you say influenced your early life—not just in music but you as a person?

JB: I lived a lot of my early life in my head and in my imagination. I read and read and read. I would go to the library every Saturday, take out about four or five books and have read them all by the middle of the week and do it all again the following Saturday. We didn't have a television in the household for most of my childhood until I was about twelve so that would have had a lot to do with it—I found out later my parents had one until I was about three which accounts for a few vague recollections of children's programmes like 'Bod' (very memorable theme tune!), but then it broke and they weren't in a rush to replace it. My parents kept to themselves and as there was no extended family around either, my social life was pretty much all in school and after-school clubs, so reading all those books was my way of learning about the world. It allowed me to explore unknown worlds and fired up my imagination—I think I must have written about as many stories as I was reading. Those beginnings also made me get used to being comfortable with my own company, because reading and creating on my own is something I know well from a young age.

When I was about five, Mum offered me the choice between joining my sister at *Brownies* or having piano lessons—after two weeks at *Brownies* it was clear I'd made the wrong choice and so I started piano lessons which was much more my thing as it turned out. Then after a few years of learning my way around the piano a little bit, I discovered there was nothing to stop me from making up little things on my own. I had a keyboard in my room at the time and I remember loving the world of possibilities that opened up and dreaming of being a composer when I grew up. I was learning classical music and had no idea what a chord even was at that stage so I was literally just playing around, but I remember how much I loved it.

Around the time I started piano lessons, we moved to a big house—it needed everything done to it including putting in a central heating system and we were briefly its caretakers huddling together like penguins in one or two rooms before other people could come along and renovate it I guess. But the garden was brilliant and next door we found some wonderful neighbours—there was a very sweet little girl who was quite a bit younger than us and her gorgeous older brother and we got to know them over the garden fence and then soon most weekends my sister and I were spending a lot of time at their house. It was always like going on holiday—at their house it was warm, there was a television, a swimming pool, there were other visitors dropping round and I remember the Mum was very glamorous. They were very generous to us and included us a lot in their family life in the house which was wildly different from ours. We would have little concerts at their house where these lovely people would patiently listen to grueling beginner violin pieces to help us prepare for music exams.

I don't remember when exactly but at some point, the keyboard disappeared out of my room and a piano appeared in the lounge. It was amazing to have a real piano to play but it took me a long, long time to realize what I'd lost—the privacy to keep making up little things without a lot of protest from either my sister or Mum. They just wanted to hear things that were finished, or at least something close to a finished performance—definitely not the fumbling beginnings of something that was yet to be formed! I didn't realize that the privacy to create had been so important to me so I didn't know to say anything and gradually I got more and more depressed without really realizing why. It wasn't until I left home that I found that privacy again.

I'm not sure what made Mum come up with the idea of us having music lessons apart from wanting to give my sister and I the opportunity to experience things she hadn't had the chance to. Mum is quite extreme though, she never learnt an instrument and seemed to actively dislike listening to music so the three cassettes on permanent rotation in Dad's car couldn't help but be pretty influential. Luckily the three cassettes were Paul Simon's *Graceland*, Elvis Presley's greatest hits and Michael Jackson's *Thriller*. I have to admit I was never a huge Elvis fan but the other two albums went in deep for sure. Besides those and the classical music I was learning on the piano and the violin, the other big musical influences on me early on were coming from watching

Top of the Pops religiously every week and taping the Top 40 on a Sunday evening. It was endlessly exciting, I think it was a really rich time in popular music culture as well, Sade, Neneh Cherry, The Police, The Eurhythmics, Chaka Kahn, early U2 were among my favourites.

Can you tell me what drew you to jazz?

JB: I got my first introduction to jazz through going to jazz dance classes as a child through into being a young adult. I spent a lot of time doing dance classes growing up, much more than music in fact. Ballet, tap, contemporary, I had a go at them all but jazz dance was my favourite. Jazz dance isn't always danced to jazz music but occasionally the teacher would pick out some things that really stuck in my mind, one of which was *Weather Report's* 'Birdland'. Such an exciting piece of music and totally unlike anything I'd ever heard. Around the same time, I heard *Blue Light 'til Dawn* by Cassandra Wilson on what was then the new radio station *JazzFM* and it was a real head-turner for me hearing somebody sing like that. The freedom in the music, the languid beat, I don't know, it just spoke to me and I went towards it. Now that I'm making my own music I can look back and see what seeds were planted then that have rooted me in my own sense of music. What I've always loved about jazz is the truth that the music speaks of. The music demands a realness which is often not there in day-to-day life. You know there's so much bullshit we have to wade through. So the honesty of the jazz art-form, how it challenges everyone within it to find their own voice and speak authentically through their instrument is something I listen to jazz for and strive to achieve.

I was about ten years old when I found I loved singing and that it was something that people responded well to. From that point on I just joined the school choir and you know I always loved to sing with gusto so at some point the music teacher noticed my efforts. You could really tell she was passionate about music and that it really mattered and that in itself was a huge gift. She gave up her time several lunch-times to encourage me to sing out even more. I remember we would go to the empty school hall and she would stand at one end and I would be at the other end and she would coax me to fill the hall with my voice. After that, she would give me solos in the school concerts and with her encouragement I just kind of did it. Then there was an English teacher who loved madrigals and he would get me singing all these old English paeans in assembly totally unaccompanied and I think through these experiences singing just became part of my identity. But confusingly there were also times when my singing was rejected which I struggled to make sense of at the time—my voice would stick out and be too noticeable at times in the choir, they would suggest it was tonally a bit 'other' which meant I was left out of some things; and then at other times, I was told my singing voice didn't match my speaking voice so I couldn't play a singing and acting role in the school production but had to take a part that was one or the other. So right from then, I was getting these messages that my voice was interesting to listen to but that somehow it didn't fit in, that it was somehow problematic.

By the time I left school for College, singing was part of who I was so in some ways it wasn't a huge step for me to put myself forward when some friends said they were going to start a band. My school environment had been pretty strait-laced and old-fashioned so I hadn't found like-minded people on that front before and it was new and exciting. I was always hanging around at live gigs and there were a couple of Oxford bands making waves among the students at the time and besides, one of those musicians was a sax player I was pretty keen on and he was going to be in the band so you know, that was pretty attractive! That man was Idris Rahman who many years later is still my life partner. It turned out though that whilst I'd done a lot of performances dancing and the little singing solos in my cozy school environment, taking the step to behind the microphone in a public forum was pretty huge. It wouldn't be the first time in my life that I was up for the challenge, but the challenge was way bigger than I could foresee. Now I can acknowledge that getting behind the microphone takes a certain kind of confidence that I lacked and have had to work on and develop by just doing it. You have huge power in those moments to dominate the mood of a room and you will dominate the mood even if you're not ready to do so, so you have to be ready within yourself to understand how you are going to use that power and to use it consciously.

Meanwhile my piano-playing had really taken a backseat. I continued to learn classical piano until I was about seventeen but then after that I just stopped playing it completely for a few years. When I found my way back to it, I was in my final year at University and I rediscovered that playing piano was a great way to get headspace, just going to the practice room and finally having the privacy to make up chord progressions and play whatever I liked to hear. It was comforting and liberating but it was also a process of rebirth musically because I re-learnt the piano from the ground up by ear and these were really my first tentative steps into composition and song writing.

Can you describe how playing the piano makes you feel/what you like about it/the sounds/anything?

JB: I think on the piano you really can create the whole spectrum of the music in whatever style, so for writing and immersing yourself in a vibe it's hard to beat. With all the keys laid out, unlike on the guitar—it's totally straightforward to find the note you want, and there's loads you can do to create an appropriate sound world for anything you're writing: clustering notes for effect, using the sustain pedal or spreading out the voicings. You can use it to be all the instrumentation in one so it's a great writing tool. Maybe it's because I started the piano pretty young that I find it comforting and immersive, and a useful touchstone to help me understand my state of mind. I can really lose myself playing the piano, so it's often a little holiday from real life.

What is the music scene like in the UK and jazz in particular?

JB: Well… the music scene in the UK is notoriously difficult and notoriously exciting and vibrant. I don't know if you could have the one without the other. The UK music scene in general is particularly trend-led and the trends that take hold here travel all across the world so the stakes can be quite high in that regard. The UK is also a society where all the 'isms' are in evidence. Ageism, sexism, racism all exist and of course the music scene is a microcosm of that.

One thing, I find quite different in the UK from other countries where I play is that the question of genre is vastly different here than elsewhere. The markers between genres here can be like canyons whereas elsewhere all that stuff is much more fluid. But as soon as you get onto this topic then you quickly start getting into the intersectionality of how the scene here works. If you are young, it's a totally different ball-game. You can mix up the genres any which way you like if you are young enough to be classified as essentially a youthful 'pop' act. Right now, there's a whole scene of young UK jazz instrumentalists invigorating British pop music and blurring the lines between the two in new exciting ways bringing in influences from grime, hip hop, afrobeat, synthwave, fusion and loads more. Older practitioners aren't relevant to this current wave as part of the story relies upon the idea that jazz was dead and boring before this generation invented it, and the 'new-ness' is important from a buzz perspective and if you're older it's hard to come across as 'new' for obvious reasons. Having said that there's always exceptions and there are one or two recently formed bands made up of slightly older male musicians that dress young that have harnessed that little bit of newness to ride the current wave alongside the twenty-somethings.

But the current wave doesn't include any vocal-led projects. I think the roots in that lie in the fact that the UK has a particularly uncomfortable relationship with what it means to be a jazz singer. For most of the music-listening public, if the music is fronted by a jazzy-sounding voice, by which I mean a voice that's kind of intimate, confessional, characterized by idiosyncratic inflections, expressive in the moment and more expressive and fluid in its delivery than your average pop singer, then the music is going to be thought of as jazz no matter what the backing is. But mostly in the UK jazz industry it seems to be a thing that if you're not explicitly scatting, and preferably over a song you haven't written, then you're open to endless discussions regarding whether or not it is jazz in a way that just doesn't come up in other countries. Often it feels like the act of writing your own song simultaneously disqualifies a person from the genre from the UK perspective.

When I look at who the wider UK music industry embraces in terms of jazzy vocalists writing their own material, they are generally American or if they're British and bringing in other genres then they need to be young enough to qualify as a 'pop' act with deep pockets behind them so that then their jazziness is marketed as only part of the package. Maybe it was always so, the great vocal legends of jazz that we know about were all the pop music of their day after all and were all American where the music originated. In conclusion, it seems like not a lot has changed.

How did your involvement with the F-IRE collective[42] affect your path?

---

42   F-IRE Collective—a creative music community founded by Barak Schmool in London. The Collective also has a record label. In July 2004, F-IRE Collective won the BBC Jazz Award for Innovation.

JB: My musical life in London got off to a wild start through meeting Robert Mitchell at one of the first jam sessions I went to. I got up and sang something like 'God bless the Child' and afterwards he asked me to join his band. I went away and listened to his music and told him I couldn't really join his band as I didn't know anything about anything and it sounded insanely complex coming from where I was coming from. Musically I was operating entirely on instinct and his music seemed very technical. Somehow or other he managed to persuade me to join the band anyway. But not having studied jazz music or composition in any formal way, and his music being so incredibly challenging, it was the huge, huge learning curve that had scared me from the outset. There I was in this band with the piano genius that is Robert, doing all manner of songs in crazy time signatures; but also with the likes of Barak Schmool who would go on to create what would become the *F-IRE Collective* and who was also a teacher at the *Royal Academy of Music* so I couldn't have been more in at the deep end—it was a very unique and personalized course of study!

Around the same time I'd also met Jonny Phillips, a guitarist with whom I co-wrote many of the songs on my first album and he'd already introduced me to many of the other band-leaders who were in the *F-IRE Collective* so that by the time I joined their ranks I had already worked with many of them. Seb Rochford who was the drummer in my band for around thirteen years, and the cellist Ben Davis who features on my debut release were both already in my band. When Barak invited me to join, I was about to release the album of songs I had written with Jonny so I think Barak thought it made sense for me to be brought in more formally. Through joining the collective I got to know a lot of other great musicians coming through—Leo Taylor, Dave Okumu, Pete Wareham, Nick Ramm, Ingrid Laubrock, Tom Arthurs, it was an exciting time. I was the only singer.

After a couple of years during which we did a great *Contemporary Music Network* tour with a bespoke *F-IRE Collective* big band of band-leaders for which we all put forward a song and arranged it for the rest of the musicians, I took the decision to leave the fold because I realized I was chasing a musical simplicity that was the opposite of the collective's avant-garde musical agenda and so it felt increasingly like we were on different paths. It felt like the audiences I was presenting my music to in that context were expecting a kind of complexity that I wasn't interested in giving them, so it just stopped feeling right.

I definitely learnt a lot from everyone and gained a lot of confidence as a musician so I completely treasure that period of my development. It's good to have had those experiences, they broadened my horizons as a musician and made me hone in on what I was striving for.

How do you find the difference playing large and small events? Do you have a preference?

JB: I've played in a lot of different contexts and you have to be on your toes to handle them all. Certain situations need more banter and others need less for example. I don't have a preference for large or small events, but what I notice more is the difference between indoor and outdoor events. When you're indoors, the silences matter more and I like the intensity and focus that is brought to the situation and you can play around with those a little within the music which adds another dimension. Bigger indoor spaces just increase the intensity of the silences so you can totally still get across an intimate feeling in a huge space. Everything always hinges on having great sound on stage and front of house. The biggest shows I have done have been open air which is a whole different scenario as the lack of walls affects the cohesion of the instruments and so it changes the whole feel of what you're creating. It can have the effect of emptying out the music when it's not in the hands of a really good sound engineer.

Are there events in your life which have affected your music? Do you think going through major events in life are useful/good for musicians or do they make you close down emotionally?

JB: I think it would be weird if my music wasn't affected by events in my life given that what I'm mainly trying to do with my music is communicate my truth. There are some times when a particular song feels unbearably raw to sing and if I don't think I can manage it then I'll leave it off the set-list, but mostly I try to open myself up to the possibility of conveying all of human emotion as I see the role of artist as one of being a conduit for that. A few years ago, I had to go on tour the week after my sister passed away and that was very, very difficult. But music is healing and whilst it felt like an outer body experience at times, ultimately sharing emotion is what I do and whilst I didn't speak about what had happened, I held her in my thoughts, sang my heart out and that felt good.

Do you feel there is still a harder path for women in jazz music? Is this changing and do you see a future where gender will not be an issue? Is the UK more difficult for women than elsewhere do you feel?

JB: I think things are improving in general which is encouraging, but it's still challenging to be female in jazz and in music in general. You can just see it at first glance on the festival line-ups, the number of female band-leaders versus the number of male band-leaders represented. Then also paths vary depending on if you're fronting your own project, if you're a sideman or sidewoman and if you're an instrumentalist or a vocalist and then how old you are and whether you're fulfilling an existing stereotype or challenging the stereotype in terms of how your music interacts with your ethnicity.

It would be wonderful if society could get to a place of equality and of mutual acceptance and mutual celebration in life in general and in the world of jazz therefore as well. Often you find that promoters, radio producers, gate-keepers, label bosses *et cetera* fall into a pattern of raising up those who chime the most with their own backgrounds and who they are as people. It's human nature, it's instinctive. So, I think real change relies upon changing the people who rise to the positions of being the gate-keepers; and right across all sectors there is a lack of diversity represented at the very top of organizations and that is at the root of many of the problems. The UK doesn't always recognize it, but it is one of the more sexist, ageist and racist countries in what we call the 'western' world.

Can you see changes happening in jazz music—are audiences growing, is there a thirst for more adventure in music do you feel?

JB: There is a thirst in general for real connection to people in the real world as a consequence of us living our lives more and more on the internet. Audiences for live music are growing in general whilst attention spans for recorded music are decreasing as we are all on our smart phones and open to so many distractions. I think the thirst is for events where crowds of people can get together and share an experience and that will always be there—live music provides a uniquely bonding emotional experience that at its best is a profound spiritual experience. It can be so powerful. But added to that, jazz music is adventurous by nature and once you tune into the spontaneity and feel the energy it can be a wild trip. At the moment it feels like there is more appetite for that than there has been for a while. Jazz music is such a 'real' art-form that gets its lifeblood from truth and authenticity. It's nice to imagine more people being drawn to it as a backlash against this age of increased fakery.

If you could meet your younger self—just about thinking of a career in jazz music, is there any piece of advice you might give her?

JB: The music is one thing, making a career out of it is something else. Everyone has their own agenda, make sure yours stays firmly focused on the music. The music business is like the Wild West so literally anything goes. Keep your wits about you but don't be afraid at the same time—and know that it won't always be easy to strike that balance. You will need to know where your limits are and to learn how to look after yourself, and to comprehensively understand yourself. Never bother comparing yourself with any other artist because there's only ever going to be one of you. At times you'll be exhausted, but always remember that being an artist is challenging on every front and that is a constant—that's the job description. Take the time to recharge if you're depleted, you are not in any other race but the human race—you get to set your own pace. But no matter what happens, your voice is as important as everyone else's—believe it, honour it and treasure your gut instinct like your best friend.

Given a blank canvas, just Julia looking at the listening and interested world, what would you like to say to people who listen, come to gigs and buy your music?

JB: Thank you for listening, I love the feeling that we are in conversation and that you would take the time to listen. You are adventurers through emotional landscapes with me because we are all wandering and wondering souls searching the music for the answers to the questions we carry within. I want to say to all of you who have got in touch over the years or come to chat after a show, I never tire of hearing your reactions. And if you have ever bought my music or come to a concert, you have directly enabled me to continue this life of enquiry as an artist and allowed me the means to carry on trying to be my best self, I am deeply grateful. When we are together in the room, the energy you bring is a part of the music and it connects with everybody present—there is nobody who could not connect with us as part of the music. Life is so full of people creating cliques and finding reasons to exclude anyone who isn't 'fill-in-the-blanks' enough, let's do our best to remember how frail and human we all are and remember we are all included.

Kitty La Roar

"The pleasure in improvisation is the leap of faith into the unknown rather than a calculation and I like the freedom within the conventions. I start by understanding why a certain piece gets to me and then store it away in a part of my mind for later."

Kitty La Roar is a British singer and drummer who was born in Bangor, Wales and moved to Bolton where she grew up. She moved to London and studied drama and theatre arts at *Goldsmiths College*. In 2004, she met jazz pianist Nick Shankland and the pair embarked together on a career in cabaret and burlesque. They gained a weekly residence at *Two2Much*, the notorious nightclub on the site of the legendary *Raymond Revue Bar* which went on to become *Soho Revue Bar* and ultimately *The Box*. Later, they performed each Thursday at the *Cellar Door* in Covent Garden where they hosted their long-running and very successful "Mashup" show. In 2008, they released 'Lucky Victims' featuring Sam Burgess on bass, Pete Wareham and Jamie Anderson on saxophones, and Simon Lea on drums. In 2010, Kitty began playing the ukulele and, with Stu Richie on drums, a trio was formed, *The Honky Tonk Cats*. During a gig, Kitty took over on drums and found she had a talent for them so drums became part of their performance as well as vocals and their other instruments. They also moved exclusively to jazz. In 2011, Kitty had a role created for her in a big band show featuring the music of Frank Sinatra. She sang alongside UK singer Kevin Fitzsimmons and they were backed by the *Pete Long Orchestra*. They incorporated music from Peggy Lee, Marilyn Monroe and Ella Fitzgerald.

Kitty and Nick performed with saxophone player Ed Jones and they went down a treat at the *London Jazz Platform* in 2017 and I have seen them play several times at different locations. They are pure entertainment.

Since 2013 Nick and Kitty have been regular performers at *Scarfe*'s bar, often adding guest musicians to their line- up. They have also travelled around the world performing, including shows in Bali, Singapore, Norway, Cuba, Damascus and more, adding performing on the Orient Express en route to Lake Como in Italy.

The Kitty La Roar Interview

Who would you say influenced your early life—not just in music but you as a person?

KL: In my early life one person stands out. I have known this person since before I was born, my twin sister Budley (her nickname). Being an identical twin is magical and yes people ask the usual, 'are you psychic?' In the past I would have smiled and sighed. You have no idea how many times she has stepped on my foot, we have bumped, knocked, accidentally hit and lost each other. But I can't deny a certain feeling of spooky action at a distance.

Back then music was dark and mysterious. I remember discovering micro-tuning with her when we were little. Of course, we didn't call it that (to us it was the rapid, banging, singy thing that made our eyes widen). There was a big smile on my face when I first heard Meredith Monk, *Volcano Songs, Duets, Lost Wind* (from the album 'Volcano Songs' (ECM 1997)).

The two of us had a common fight despite relentless comparison and competition. As a unit we felt part of something bigger than one and it had a profound impact. Being ensemble just felt right and now I never underestimate the value of shared time and experience. It's the same phenomenon as the knowing of someone's tendencies in jazz because when you play with someone for a long time, you flow together. Patterns fall into sympathy and you'll do the same thing at the same time, that's very similar to a 'spooky' twin thing.

I'll admit that when it comes to 'self' I struggle to see a singular and I prefer a collection of multiple faces/egos. Probably why I'm quite cozy as Kitty LaRoar and I'm quite glad it's a name that jumps out of a playbill. Imagine being called 'twinnie' right through to the age of twelve. We had special relationships with teachers through music and although we undertook no formal training it was something that gave us what all kids crave; attention and praise. Singing felt good and it was just what we did. It was our thing.

Why jazz music? Can you describe how performing makes you feel/ what you like about it /the sounds/anything?

KL: I like melodies and lines that make turn your head and sit still to fathom. Notes that leap out of nowhere, toss back your head and make you grin (like the joyous yell on 'Stella by Starlight: My Funny Valentine Miles Davis in Concert'). There's a wonderfully frustrating struggle in learning bebop heads by ear and picking up the grammar of Charlie Parker. Jazz has such expression and commitment in its performance. For instance, I love this description, "King Coleman Hawkins plays the saxophone. It is not the usual note of the saxophone he produces, but a quiet note which he maintains in amazing convolutions of sound, appearing as though he would die of the effort rather than give up."[43] Every time I read that I smile.

For me jazz has that physical commitment with spirit. As soon as I found out what that type of music was called, I wanted to hear more and I count myself lucky to feel so excited by jazz. I never feel intimated by a lack of technical knowledge. The pleasure in improvisation is the leap of faith into the unknown rather than a calculation and I like the freedom within the conventions. I start by understanding why a certain piece gets to me and then store it away in a part of my mind for later.

It definitely is an emotional response and it's really hard to describe why a performance can be so affecting, but there's a Goldilocks zone of chops, passion and meaning. It's a moment of everything coming together that you really want to go back to because you've been somewhere and it feels like time has stopped and the music exists as a thing with a distinct and independent existence.

As a singer you really notice the change in lyrics in jazz. With some songs, as they are products of their age, the racial and gender tones can be problematic. Some of these issues never occurred to me when I was younger. Are we becoming more aware? Perhaps. Many of the lyrics are just so witty,

---

43 *Orchestra and Variety—The Manchester Guardian, DF Boyd, 26 June 1934.*

beautiful and right. 'The Folks Who Live on the Hill' (Jerome Kern/Oscar Hammerstein) has the line "our veranda will command a view of meadows green, the kind of view that really wants to be seen". It captures a sense of a yearning for a pastoral idyllic that you find in a lot of the songs of *The American Songbook*. Think of Hoagy Carmichael too. It's like jazz music enables a poetry and impressionism that seems to sit somewhere between classical and folk, the sophisticated and colloquial, and really is at its finest and most enjoyable juxtaposed.

How do you feel about young people and jazz? Do you feel there is still the interest there was a few years ago or is this growing? Do you think education—jazz degrees etc. are making a difference?

KL: I think young people are very conscious of the time they are living in and behaviours are jazz-like; rich in inverted commas and quotes. I know what you're thinking—every generation has contemporary youth movements—but there's a self-awareness and control today that feels different.

Is it a simplification to say an apocalyptic ticking clock has enforced maturity? I'm not sure, but I see a strong sense of focus in young people, the sense of creating their own futures, defining success in their own terms because channels for education and expression are being shut down or have become too expensive.

I did a Drama and Theatre Arts Degree at *Goldsmith's College* London in the late 90s and I remember chatting about grants and loans with a twinkly-eyed lecturer who said in the 70's they all had grants and they spent a lot of it on champagne! Me—the 70's hmmm? Champagne, really, Champagne? It evokes a time when you could study a humanities degree without the pressure of getting a vocational qualification. Things seem very different now.

Jazz degrees may seem absurd to some and I can see where they are coming from, arguing jazz is empirical. They do have an effect on a scene and you can hear the syllabuses in song choices at the late session jams at Ronnie Scott's. In my mind it's great to have so many talented people loving the same music you do and pursuing a life in music is hard and I take my hat off to anyone who has chosen a life as a pro jazz musician. Choosing such a degree is a serious statement. Of course, if it's in your blood—'tis no choice really.

I wonder if the courses live up to expectations. After all you don't need a degree if you want to make a living gigging or teaching privately. It does create a new way of talking about jazz though, shot through with all the pros and cons of academia. Universities as an equivalent to conservatories though? I wonder how many hours of training are possible when students have several part-time jobs to support themselves.

Jazz-fusion (hip hop/RnB/Electronica) probably means there's a whole new world of listeners to jazz (Yup, I know you're thinking, 'fusion? 1970-80's'). I like it, if it gets me. The word grassroots comes up a lot in mainstream media with musicians setting up their own scenes and using social media seems to be identified as the driver. Whether it is real or authentic seems like the wrong question as opposed to, "How much is being cut from arts and music education?" I'd like to think education could be an open door throughout our lives and that fairer access could prevent a degree from being nothing more than an expensive members' badge. We could all enter our learning as 'Education—still in progress' (Tony Benn).

Have you noticed a change in demographics at gigs—and is this different in the UK and elsewhere?

KL: There are many types of gig for a singer like me: there are concerts, festivals and then there are bread and butter bar/hotel gigs. I'm lucky enough to do a wide variety.

In bars and hotels even though I'd have thought it obvious I'm having the time of my life the sympathetic question of, "Do you have a day job?" comes up as often as, "What are you doing playing here? You should be on a big stage!" It kind of tells you everything you need to know. Certainly, on the London scene in the past five years there has been a move by hotels and bars to offer live jazz that is a world away from safe cocktail piano swing/pop covers. More like a 1930s club, they offer a half-way house to a club/concert atmosphere, albeit accompanied by expensive cocktails.

At concerts and festivals there's none of that randomness and ambiguity and the demographic of the audience has always been quite mixed. I love gigging and it's unique and humbling to build a rapport with people who love jazz. I don't think it's a case of the demographic being older or younger, richer/poorer, but how cities and towns are different. I'm based in London and have seen a lot of musicians moving away. One of the pleasures of travelling to play is seeing how much enthusiasm there is for jazz—it's our club! I loved playing at *Derry Jazz Festival* and admired the balance of local performance and ticketed events.

You often collaborate with different musicians—I have seen you play with saxophonists, bass players, trumpeters and violinists. What makes you decide to ask someone to collaborate with you?

That's an interesting question. Running a residency is wonderful thing sometimes as you necessarily are in a position to invite a range of different players. I hear people at jams or see them play with someone I know and check them out. As you get to know people you hear their uniqueness more and what first drew your ear is developed. The choices they make, the openness of their expression and the emotions are big factors. It's a real pleasure hearing people think, especially if you minimize arrangements in favour of improvisation.

That being the case, there's a certain amount of largesse involved, very much dependent on personality. When you get to chat if there's not much camaraderie then you kind of know, but talented musicians who are lovely people are inspirational. Outside the residency there are musicians who I have known for years and we have a different kind of bond when recording and performing original music. Then it's intense and you are asking for much more. On "Valentines Eve" I collaborated with Nick Shankland (piano) and Ed Jones (tenor sax). You yourself Sammy, said of Ed's playing on "Ebb and Flow" (from his *Album for Your Ears Only 2019*) "The sax then enters and Jones adds his magic, bringing the total freewheeling aspect into an almost coherent format. At the same time, he maintains that wonderful sense of freedom, which only the very experienced players can combine". I totally agree and I loved recording with Ed and Nick because we gave each other loads of room to do what felt right on the day. There's a lot of trust and love in that kind of playing.

I have spoken to you when there have been personal events happening in your life. Do you think these affect the music or your performance? How?

It's a thing to express a song with authenticity. I used to think it was like acting. About crafting an emotional journey onto a song. Now I think the emotions and meanings within music have their own power if you are open to them. In heighten states of shock and grief, everything becomes more significant and shinier.

When my mother died three years ago it was a watershed moment and I think I'm a different person now, I remember a close friend staying you can see amongst our peers who has lost a parent. It leaves an indelible mark. A dear friend Gordon, passed away last Christmas, way too early at forty-three and it felt impossible to sing. On the first night back I sang outside my skin and relished being alive. You do it for them and because you can't hide. I imagine my mother and Gordon in the stage light. You can tell I was a kid brought up on Spielberg films! It feels like we are together again sometimes.

Music is the externalization of such deeply personal events and it makes expression authentic and the vulnerability is okay because you know the audience understand and have been through it themselves.

Do you feel there is still a harder path for women in jazz music? Is this changing and do you see a future where gender will not be an issue?

KL: I think there are two elements to this. The first is much more visible, the objectification of women as performers in a male dominated scene. The second is a more pervasive gender bias that you find in all walks of life.

I've always been attracted to the glamour and humour of a self-constructed bombshell figure. There's something unexpectedly gender neutral and defiantly camp about it. It makes me smile to think of Mae West insisting the studio hired Duke Ellington and his orchestra to accompany her ('My Old Flame') in the film 'Belle of The Nineties'. I like the heightened theatre of it. I think a lot of people don't get it though and equate it with exploitation. Is a more glamorous appearance a tradeoff for getting to do more of the music you want to do? Perhaps but I would like to think it didn't matter. Are male performers subject to the same criticism? Who would ever criticize a tie as an overtly phallic piece of clothing? No one right?

Do male musicians make it harder for women in jazz? Well there have been occasions when the male members of a band are glad for a gig that is booked because there is a female singer co-fronting the show but are disparaging backstage. Fortunately, I have had very few of those experiences. When it did happen in a big band show I was doing, I got the feeling there was little regard for the show and it was a symptom of that. Amongst jazz musicians I don't find gender to be an issue between us at all. The stories of children, relationships and the challenges of work that could be associated with women, I hear from men in the world of jazz.

I'm more concerned about the lean towards the right online and in politics as a sign of things becoming harder for women. In *Invisible Women: Exposing Data Bias in a World Designed for Men* by Caroline Criado Perez, a deep-knit gender bias is evident in how society designs and builds. Form and function are based on the male body and don't take into account the female body. I think this, as Perez's calls it "one-size-fits-men" is unconsciously felt to be the "right" universalization. It's really fascinating when asking the question why many women's lives are "harder". It widens the debate beyond definitions of discrimination that blames individual behaviour.

It makes my heart sink how often on social media, when gender issues crop up, how quickly the remarks can get quite toxic. I've often found that what lies behind derogatory uses of "feminist" and "femininazi" is really a bias against the left. Let's just say there's a hell of a lot of that online! I do enjoy Twitter because you can reach so many interesting people who love jazz, but I do worry about the future in relation to female voices online. In his book *Clear Bright Future* Paul Mason states "in the few short years since social media became a global reality—violent misogyny has become a pervasive subcultural identifier for the far right worldwide." I feel like in politics today, the far right has a huge mainstream presence. It's a new thing to be aware of as much as Perez's analysis of data can provide new insights for the future of gender issues.

I know you perform a lot with your husband Nick Shankland and also Budley. How important is it for you to have support of your family and does your work affect your personal life?

I don't see a lot of distinction between my work and personal life. 'Lucky bugger' doesn't even cover it. So many people have to make choices between the two usually at the expense of their personal happiness. Married jazz musicians are nothing new and I suspect the understanding of the ups and downs is key and more than that there's a trust and connection. For me and Nick, the gigs came first and then the romance, so jazz is the food of love or we are just really lazy!

My twin sister Budley is a massive source of inspiration and compassion and I honestly don't know what I would do without her. She manages to balance so many things as a musician and a mother and teaches me a lot about being a woman in jazz. Doing a gig with her is so much fun, we have a range of instant communication looks from "that was sweeeeeeet" to "the only way to improve this gig is to take off and nuke it from orbit".

A while back you began to play snare drum and now use it extensively in your performances. What made you do this and how has having an instrument been with the performances?

Believe me, there are times at gigs when I look down at my drum and ask myself, "how the hell did this happen?" It all started when I played in a trio with Nick and Stu Ritchie.

Stu is a jazz drummer who fell in love with the ukulele and became a fiend! He's a creative and mischievous musician who will delve into a stick bag mid solo and produce a wind-up marching toy to place on the skin. We got a trio together expressly to play ukulele, with piano, vocals and his unique drum kit. It was a real hoot, me comping, Stu with a ukulele and one time when Stu put his brushes down to play a solo, I picked up the brushes and played the drum. It kind of happened naturally and I never really set out with the intention of playing drums. I'm sure jazz drummers tear their hair out seeing my kit, it's an orchestral snare stand with a Gretsch brass snare, attached two boom arms with (to the right) a ride rivet cymbal and (to the left) two splashes mounted as a closed hi-hat.

I have a love/hate relationship with the kit because it's great as a female singer to be so physical and as part of the rhythm section central to the music in performance. However, hearing yourself as a singer is quite a challenge and I'm often kicking myself for forgoing the subtleties of voice alone. I get to scat and accent swerves with rhythm and I'm more than happy to admit I trade technical skill for swing and crazy feel.

If you could meet your younger self—just about thinking of a career in

music, is there any piece of advice you might give her?

I think I would say when it comes to choices at G.C.S.E pick music instead of drama! We could only choose one arts subject. I'm with Jean Luc Picard on this one though, life is a tapestry and if you pick away at one thread the whole fabric could unravel.

Given a blank canvas, just Kitty looking at the world, what would you like to say to people who listen, come to gigs and buy your music?

I think like many people I am my own worst critic and I remember a time in the past when perhaps I might never have had the courage to perform jazz. When I sing for people who appreciate and support what I'm doing, it's like they lend you courage and inspiration. A circle becomes complete and a solo voice in my head becomes a chorus. The music wouldn't exist or make sense without you and what we create belongs to you and me.

EPILOGUE

It has been an enormous privilege and pleasure to interview the women in this book. The thought they gave to the questions I asked was profound and their responses inspirational. As well as the many differences, much common ground was found in these interviews: the importance of giving your very best consistently, the compulsion to make music and how music allows you to 'just be' in the moment, communicating with others whether they are playing or listening. There seems to be agreement that more female role models are needed in the industry and that you don't become a jazz musician by going to music school and taking a jazz degree. This may help, but the real education is gained by working in the industry. The passion for the music is clear from each woman and there is an unrelenting positivity which is catching and undeniable.

I was struck also by the humility and candour of many of these amazing stars of jazz music. Many of the women thanked me for including them in the book, for not changing the meaning of their words and for giving them a platform to speak freely. These were women who I had approached, not really expecting them to be able to find time for me or to give such extensive answers to my questions. The trust they gave me was humbling.

What struck me most of all was the absolute dedication of these women to their music and the relationships they have with their instrument or voice, the audience and collaborators on stage. The interviews were a constant learning curve and every woman had another element to add, an extra gift to jazz music and our understanding of just what drives musicians.

You can find more on each woman online and there are many more sources where you can find more about jazz music on the internet, in books and printed media. I think one of the most profound lessons in the interviews is how broadly jazz arms can spread and how welcoming they can be. If you find the right people, the right music and the right space—then, who knows what can happen?

Index

Lightning Source UK Ltd.
Milton Keynes UK
UKHW010720070223
416609UK00002B/797